SCHOOL APPLICATIONS AND APPEALS EXPLAINED

J. TOMLINSON

J. TOMLINSON

Copyright © 2016 J. TOMLINSON

ISBN-13: 978-1530714469

ISBN-10: 153071446X

Forward

This book is School Applications Explained and the bestselling School Appeals Explained combined together into one book.

Both books provide clear information on their subjects, however bringing them both together into this book creates a comprehensive guide to anyone who is interested in Admissions and Admission Appeals in England.

School Applications Explained gives detailed information on the system of school place allocations and was originally intended for those parents who were preparing to apply for a school place. However it does cover some aspects of the allocation system in more detail which readers who are preparing for an Admission Appeal may find useful, both in understanding why they weren't offered a place at the school they wanted and in understanding what they should do next.

School Appeals Explained gives an overview of the allocation system and then provides information for parents who are considering or preparing an Admission Appeal for a place at the school that they want.

Both books are reproduced here in their entirety as originally published as single books, therefore there will be some duplication in the appendices and glossary.

SCHOOL APPLICATIONS EXPLAINED

J. TOMLINSON

Copyright © 2015 J. Tomlinson

All rights reserved.

ISBN-13: 978-1518774225
ISBN-10: 1518774229

CONTENTS

Introduction

1	How School Places are Allocated	1
2	Applications and Allocation Timetable	Pg 5
3	Oversubscription Criteria	Pg 9
4	Oversubscription Criteria Examples	Pg 15
5	Case Studies	Pg 31
6	Common Assumptions Made by Parents	Pg 55
7	Summer Born Children	Pg 69
8	Preparing to Apply	Pg 75
9	Applying for a School Place	Pg 87
10	What to do if you didn't get the Place you wanted	Pg 95
11	In-Year Applications	Pg 105
	Glossary	Pg 110

Introduction

This book is for anyone who will be applying for a school place for their child in England. The book explains how school places are allocated. Whilst the book is largely aimed at people applying for a place for their child to start Primary or Secondary School, there is also information about applying for a school place at other times such as if you have moved into another area or feel that your child needs to change school. The information in this book will help parents and carers increase their chances of a successful school application.

In my work as a School Appeals Clerk, I have seen so many parents come to appeal because they did not understand how the system for allocating school places worked. If they had known more about it, many of them would not have needed to come to appeal as they would have got a place at a school they were happy with. Often parents assume that they will automatically get into the school that they put on their application, but unfortunately this does not always happen.

This book aims to give the reader an understanding of how the school admission system works; covering the law around School Admissions, the role of the Local Education Authority; how different places are allocated differently for different schools; what to research before applying for school places and how to maximise your chances of a successful application. The book also gives examples of common mistakes or assumptions that parents can make in the application process which can make the difference between securing a place at a school they would be happy with or not because they did not understand the system. There is also vital information about what to do if your application is not successful and you are not offered a place at a school you would wish your child to attend. Knowing what to do in this situation is crucial and can mean that a place at an acceptable school is secured without the need to go to appeal.

1 HOW SCHOOL PLACES ARE ALLOCATED

Summary

All children starting either Primary or Secondary School need to have an application made by their parents or carers to get a place at a school. Applications are made in Autumn / Winter to start school in the following September. More than one school can be put on the application for a school place and there are strict deadlines for the whole process, from when the applications open to when the offers of school places are made. This process is called the normal admission round.

All Schools have a certain number of children which they are allowed to accept. If less children than this apply in the normal admission round, then all the children must be offered a place. If there are more children applying than there are places, not all of the children would be offered a place at the School. Different Schools have different ways of determining which children would be offered a place in this situation. These are called oversubscription criteria and form part of the School's Admission Arrangements. The School Admissions Code 2014 requires that all schools have oversubscription criteria.

Applications for a school place at a time different to the normal admission round, such as if you have moved area and your child needs a place at a local school, are called In Year applications. These are dealt with differently and there is a separate chapter on In Year applications later in the book.

How School Places are allocated

The principal law governing the allocation of school places is the School Admissions Code 2014. This sets out

what the law says Local Education Authorities and Admission Authorities have to do, as well as giving examples of what they can choose to do in terms of their admission arrangements.

Things that have to be done include complying with the specific timetable for applications, and ensuring that certain children (in specific criteria) are automatically admitted to a school in the normal admission round. Examples of what they can choose to do include a selection of different criteria that could be used to give some children a higher priority than other applicants for example children of teaching staff. Admission Authorities can then choose which if any of these suggested categories they would use in their own Admission Arrangements, or devise their own as long as they comply with the requirements of the Code.

All places at schools have to be allocated using the Admission Authority's Admission Policy. Different Admission Authorities can have different Admission Policies, but there are strict rules to ensure that consultation is done in advance of any changes to these being implemented, and they have to be approved by the School Adjudicator before they come into force. The Admissions Policy must include Oversubscription Criteria which are used to rank applicants if there are more applicants than places in order to determine which applicants are offered places at the school.

An Admission Authority can be the Local Education Authority for Council run schools, or other schools, such as Academies can themselves be the Admission Authority and have their own Admissions Policy.

All schools must have a Published Admission Number which is the number of children they can admit in each year group. In the Normal Admission Round, if less children apply than there are places, they would all be allocated a place at the school. If there were more applicants than places, the oversubscription criteria are used to rank the children in order to determine which children would be allocated a place at the school.

Occasionally it is possible that it is decided to admit more than this number, but usually the Published Admission Number is the amount of children that can be admitted. If an Admission Authority decides it can admit above the PAN it must notify the Local Education Authority to enable coordination of school places in the Local Education Authority area.

Role of the Local Education Authority

The Local Education Authority is responsible for co-ordinating all of the applications in the normal admission round and sending out the final place offers. All applications to start Primary School and Secondary School are sent to them to administer. The Local Education Authority has to make sure that if an applicant would be offered a place at more than one of the schools that they have preferenced, that they are offered a place at the highest preferenced school out of the ones that they could be offered.

The Local Education Authority will also run the process of "topping up". This is where the allocations system is run at periodic intervals once children who have declined or returned places have been taken into account, and new applicants are allocated places off the waiting list. Topping up is run in the same way that the main allocations system works in that all place allocations are done in accordance with the oversubscription criteria of the school.

Admission Authority

The Admission Authority is for many schools the Local Education Authority. These schools have the Local Education Authority's admission arrangements including the oversubscription criteria. Other schools are their own Admission Authority. Applications in the normal admission round to these schools would still be made to the Local Education Authority as part of the school application. But they would then be passed to the Admission Authority of the school for them to rank the applications using their oversubscription criteria, or would be ranked by the Local Education Authority using the oversubscription criteria of the school. These rankings would then be passed back to the Local Education Authority who would co-ordinate them with all the other applications and schools. This ensures that each applicant only receives one offer of a school place on National Offer Day, and that it is for the highest preferenced school that an applicant has qualified for a place at.

2 APPLICATIONS AND ALLOCATION TIMETABLE

Summary

For applications for either Primary or Secondary School, there are set dates within the application process. These dates are when the applications for places open, the closing date for applications and the date where applicants are notified of the place they have got (National Offer Day). These are different for Primary and Secondary school applications and are specified in the legislation so that all Local Education Authorities have to work to the same date.

Local Education Authorities will have information on their website and in their literature detailing the application dates for that year. Schools that are their own admission authorities should also have this information on their websites.

It is very important to check with your Local Authority about their dates as some of these such as when applications open can vary between Local Authorities. The deadlines for applications and the dates for National Offer Day for both Primary and Secondary schools are specified in the School Admissions Code 2014.

For schools which include an assessment as part of their application process, it is very important to know the dates and deadlines involved to ensure that your child does not miss the assessment dates as for some schools this could mean they wouldn't be considered for a place.

Key Dates

There are some set dates which are specified within the School Admissions Code 2014. This means that all Local Education Authorities need to comply with them. They are the deadlines for applications and then the date on which the school offers are sent out to parents. The date on which the offers are sent out to parents is called National Offer Day. If the National Offer Day falls on a weekend, it is usually on the nearest working day but it is worth contacting your Local Education Authority to clarify when they will be sending out the information.

There are different sets of dates for Secondary School and Primary School applications, with Secondary School applications happening first in the admissions cycle. Look at your Local Education Authority's website for details about when the applications open for each admission round.

Application Dates

Secondary School Applications

Deadline for applications: 31st October

National Offer Day: 1st March*

Primary School Applications

Deadline for applications: 15th January

National Offer Day: 16th April*

---

*or the nearest working day if this date is a weekend or bank holiday

Deadlines- The Importance of applying in time

Applying on time or late could make the difference between getting a place or not at your preferred school. This means that applying on time is vital in maximising your chances of getting a place at one of the schools you have put on your application.

The reason that it is so important to apply on time is that when the places are allocated, the applications that were received on time are considered before the late applications. If a school is undersubscribed so has less people applying than there are places, then all applicants will get a place. But if a school has more applicants than places, it means that late applications will not get a look in because all the places will go to on time applications. Even if a late application would have been placed high up in the list of priorities such as for having a sibling, they would be considered after all the on time applications and therefore would miss out on a place if all the places had been allocated to on time applications, even those that would have come under a lower criteria in the oversubscription criteria.

An easier way to think about this is if a school had 80 places, if there were 80 on time applicants they would get the places and any late applications wouldn't. No matter how high a priority a late application may have under the oversubscription criteria, if they are dealt with as a late application and the places have already been allocated to on time applicants there are no places left to allocate so they wouldn't get a place.

Late applications are ranked according to the oversubscription criteria, so if there were a few places left after the on time applications, those with the highest priority would be allocated places but not all. Applicants who might have easily gained a place had they applied on time and been considered with the other on time applications may well not get a place if they apply late.

Although a child who would have a higher priority under the oversubscription criteria would be placed higher up the waiting list (which is ranked according to the oversubscription criteria), and therefore would have a better chance of being offered a place if one became available there is no guarantee that a place would become available. It is much better to apply on time so that your child is considered with the other on time applicants and their chance of getting a place is maximised.

Some Local Education Authorities have processes in place where they try to chase up families that have not submitted an application by the closing date. But this is not a statutory requirement and not all Local Education Authorities do this, so do not assume that if you miss the closing date you will be reminded. For peace of mind and to make sure that your application is dealt with alongside the others, and not as a late application you must make sure that you have submitted it by the deadline.

<u>Testing dates</u>

If you are considering a school which tests children as part of their selection process- whether that is a selective school where children have to sit a test to determine if they are eligible to be considered for a place, or a school which gives a certain number of children priority in their oversubscription criteria due to a special aptitude, it is very important to research this early on. Selective schools often hold their open evenings when children are in Year 5, and have the testing dates early in their Year 6. Schools that award places under special aptitude have varying testing times. If you want your child to participate in an assessment process, it is essential to know the assessment dates and the deadline by which they need to be registered to participate. If the testing dates are missed this means your child is likely to have missed out on the opportunity of being assessed. For selective schools this would mean they would not be considered for a place at all as these schools do not have to offer places to children who have not been through the testing process and deemed suitable, even if they are undersubscribed. For special aptitude schools, although an application can still be made, if your child has not been assessed they would not have the chance of being placed in the higher priority in the oversubscription criteria.

3 OVERSUBSCRIPTION CRITERIA

Summary

All schools have a certain number of children which they are allowed to accept for each year group. If fewer children apply than are places, then all must be offered a place at the school. But if more children apply than are places, the Admission Authority has to determine which children are offered a place. Oversubscription Criteria are what are used to determine which children will be offered a place at a school if there are more applicants than places available. All Admission Authorities must publish the Oversubscription Criteria that they use as part of their published Admission Arrangements.

This chapter gives general information about Oversubscription Criteria and how they work. The following two chapters then give example Oversubscription Criteria and Case Studies to demonstrate how they work in practice.

This chapter also explains Choice vs Preference.

Oversubscription Criteria

All Admissions Policies have set categories in which children are placed when they apply for a place. These are called Oversubscription Criteria. If there are less applicants for a school in the normal admission round than places available then all the applicants would be offered a place. However if there were more applicants than places, the oversubscription criteria would be used to determine which children were offered a place by ranking them in order of criteria. Then the places would be allocated from the top of the ranked list downwards i.e. if there were 100 applicants for 60 places, the applicants would be ranked using the criteria and the top 60 applicants in the ranked list would be offered places.

The law requires that the highest priority be given to looked after and previously looked after children. Children whose statement of special educational needs (SEN) or Education, Health and Care (EHC) plan names the school must be admitted to it. Some Admissions Policies state that these children will be admitted automatically, others list them within their oversubscription criteria as the top criteria. After these children, the oversubscription criteria must then be applied to all other applicants in the order set out in the Admissions Policy for the school.

Different schools can have different Admission Policies. Often different types of schools will have different types of oversubscription criteria. One example is faith schools which often give regular church goers a higher priority under their Admissions Policy than non-church goers, or baptised Catholics being given a higher priority than non-baptised Catholics for Catholic faith schools. Some schools ask for additional information from the parent to prove that a child should be placed in a higher criteria, for example a faith school wishing to get further information about a child's church attendance or proof of a child's baptism. If the additional information is not provided, it can mean that the child is placed in a lower criteria than the parents might have expected. This can then mean that the child doesn't get a place at the school due to being placed in a lower criteria than they would have been had information been provided to verify that they were eligible for placement in a higher criteria at the time of application.

Some commonly used criteria are listed below:

- Siblings at the School: The Admission Policy must clearly state what is considered as a "sibling" for example older brothers or sisters, half brothers or sisters, step siblings, foster siblings living at the same address but not other family members such as cousins who live at the same address. Also whether siblings at the school count for siblings in any year at the school, or only siblings in certain years. Some schools do not count children in the Sixth Form as siblings, especially if they have joined from another school. It is important to look at the Admissions Policy for any school you are interested in to ensure that you understand how their sibling criteria is applied if this is one that you think your child should be eligible for.
- Distance from the School: The Admission Policy must specify how the distance will be measured- some Authorities use a straight line distance, others use distance by road. The points that the measurement will be taken from are also specified, for example from the home address to the centre of the main school building. Many Admission Authorities have specialist mapping software which they use to determine the distances. Distance is usually used to rank children within the criteria, for example all children qualifying for sibling priority could then be ranked according to distance from the school
- Catchment Areas: This criteria is often, but not always used. They must be designed so that they are reasonable and are clearly defined. Parents who live outside the catchment area of a particular school are still able to express a preference for that school. It is important to double check if you think that a school you are interested in uses Catchment Area as one of its Oversubscription Criteria as sometimes parents think that schools use this system when they do not.
- Feeder Schools: Some Admission Authorities give priority to children attending a particular school which is named as a Feeder School. This must be clearly stated in the Admission Policy.
- Social and Medical Need: Admission Authorities using this criteria must set out clearly how they will define this need, and specify what supporting evidence would need to be submitted as proof. If in doubt it is safest to contact the Local Education Authority

well in advance of the closing date for applications to clarify the processes involved in getting a child classified under this criteria.
- Nearest school: Many Admission Authorities give a higher priority to children for whom the school is their nearest. It is important to check how this is worded as the way in which it is applied can vary between Admission Authorities. The Local Education Authority will be able to tell you your nearest school under their policies.

Choice vs Preference

When parents talk about submitting their application for a school place for their child, they often talk about "choices" they are going to put down. When Admission Authorities talk about the applications they have received for places at a school, they talk about "preferences".

Choice and Preference are not the same, and it is very important to understand the difference between the two in order to have a better understanding of how school places are allocated.

The School Admissions Code 2014 gives the parents the legal right to "express a preference" for a school which is what they do when they name the schools on their application for a school place. Parents must be allowed to name at least three schools on their application. Many Local Education Authorities allow parents to name more than three schools.

For applications in the normal admission round (starting Primary or Secondary School), the Local Education Authority co-ordinates the allocation of places and is required to offer parents a place at the highest preference school on their application at which a place is available for them. If schools are popular, and there are more applications than places, not all children will get a place at the school. This means that although sometimes parents believe that if they have put a particular school on an application, they will get a place there because they "chose" it, this is unfortunately not always the case. The determination of which children are allocated a place is done by ranking applicants according to the Oversubscription Criteria for the school. If a school is undersubscribed, and a child isn't ranked highly enough according to the Oversubscription Criteria, they won't be successful in getting a place.

Local Education Authorities must ensure, so far as is reasonably practicable, that applicants are offered places at whichever school is their highest preference at which a place is available for them. This means that if an applicant qualifies for a place at more than one of their preferences, they should be offered a place at the highest preferenced school out of the ones that they could be allocated a place at.

Unfortunately, "choosing" a school by putting it on the school application does not guarantee getting a place at that school.

4 OVERSUBSCRIPTION CRITERIA EXAMPLES

<u>Summary</u>

Different schools have different oversubscription criteria. It is very important to research and understand the oversubscription criteria of the schools that you are interested in so that you can get an idea of whether your child has a realistic chance of being offered a place. Demand changes year on year so it is never possible to predict for sure, but understanding how the system works and how the places are allocated at the school you are considering will allow you to make a more informed decision than a parent who assumes that their child will get in because they put the school on their application.

Different types of schools often have different oversubscription criteria. This chapter gives example oversubscription criteria for various different types of schools.

When looking at the oversubscription criteria for a school, it is important to read the accompanying guidance information. This will normally give more information about each priority within the oversubscription criteria such as how to request that your child is considered under the priority for medical needs (one of the higher priorities if used) or defining terms such as siblings, or clarifying the method used to measure distance. The definitions and processes vary between Local Education Authorities and individual schools so it is imperative to fully understand what is meant in the oversubscription criteria for the school which you are interested in. Contacting the individual school or Local Education Authority is always a good idea to confirm your understanding and to ensure that you know all the information which needs to be provided as part of your application.

The following chapter has Case Studies using the Oversubscription Criteria examples in this chapter. Each example states which Case Study it is used in to make it easier to find the appropriate Case Study.

Local Education Authority

These are the oversubscription criteria from a large Local Education Authority and it applies to the community and voluntary-controlled schools for which it is the Admission Authority.

Children with a statement of special educational needs will be admitted to the school named on their statement.

We will offer places to children in the following order of priority.

Priority 1

a) Children in public care or fostered under an arrangement made by the local authority.

b) Pupils without a statement but who have Special Educational Needs, or with exceptional medical or mobility needs, that can only be met at a specific school.

Priority 2

Children with older brothers or sisters who will be at school at the start of the academic year and are living at the same address . This includes priority for a sibling applying for an infant school where the older sibling is or will be attending the linked junior school.

This priority will not apply where the older sibling joined the sixth form from a different school.

Priority 3

Where children attend the following infant and junior schools they will have priority for the linked infant or junior school:

X Infant School linked to X Junior School

Should there be more children than places available priority 4 will be used as a tie break.

Priority 4

We will give priority to parents who put their nearest school (see note 6).

This does not include any voluntary-aided schools which act as their own admission authorities.

If we have more applications than there are places, we will offer places first to children living nearest to the school (measured in a straight line).

Priority 5

We will give priority to parents who choose a X (school within this Local Education Authority area) school, which is not the one nearest to their home address

If we have more applications than there are places, we will offer places first to children living nearest to the school (measured in a straight line).

This example is used for Case Study 1.

Academy

Below are oversubscription criteria for two different Academies. Both are secondary schools but there are differences in the criteria used. These could make the difference between a child getting a place or not, and this demonstrates the importance of knowing and understanding the oversubscription criteria used by the schools which you are considering. The first Academy gives sibling preference to all children who would have a sibling at the school when they started there and does not limit the year groups which the sibling at the school would need to be in to qualify under this criteria. The second Academy also gives sibling preference to children who would have a sibling at the school when they started there, but restricts this to those children whose sibling would be in Year 11 or below. This means that children who have siblings at the school that will be in year groups above Year 11 at the start of the next school year would not be granted sibling priority. This could in some cases mean that an application for a place could be unsuccessful, depending on the criteria in which the child was placed in and the distance which they lived from the school.

Example 1

i.   Criterion 1

Looked-after children and previously looked-after children. A looked-

after child is one who is either in the care of a Local Authority or who is being provided with accommodation by a Local Authority in the exercise of their social services functions (under the terms of the Children Act 1989 s 22(1)) at the time of making an application to the school. Previously looked-after children are those who were looked-after, but ceased to be so because they were adopted (under the terms of the Adoption and Children Act 2002) or became subject to a Residence Order or a Special Guardianship Order (both under the terms of the Children Act 1989).

ii.   Criterion 2

Children with exceptional medical or mobility needs which can realistically only be met by the Academy. Applications in these categories must be supported by a statement in writing from a doctor or other relevant professional. Each case will be considered on its merits.

iii.   Criterion 3

Children with brothers or sisters who are on the Academy's roll at the start of the academic year 2015-16.

iv.   Criterion 4

Children for whom The X Academy is the nearest secondary school.

v.   Criterion 5

Any other children.

3.10.   Tie break

3.10.1.   Within each criterion, if there is oversubscription, the places will be allocated according to distance. Children living closer to the Academy will, therefore, be allocated a place before those who live further away.

3.10.2.   Random allocation will be used as a tie-break in categories 2-5 above to decide who has highest priority for admission if the distance between a child's home and the Academy is equidistant in any two or more cases. This process will be overseen by an independent panel.

This example is used for Case Study 2

Example 2

Allocation of places:

i) Children who have a statement of special educational needs which names the Academy will be allocated a place.

ii) If the number of applications does not exceed the number of places available, all applicants will be granted a place at the Academy.

iii) If there are more applications than available places (oversubscription), the following oversubscription criteria will be used to allocate places:

Criteria 1

a) Children who are or have been in public care or fostered under an arrangement made by the local authority.

b) Pupils without a statement but who have special educational needs, or with exceptional medical or mobility needs, which can only reasonably be met at X Academy.

Criteria 2

Children with older brothers or sisters who will be on roll in Years 7-11 at X Academy at the start of the academic year 2015-16. We can give priority for brothers and sisters only if they are living in the same house and we receive the application by the closing date.

Criteria 3

Children who, at the time of application, are on roll at the primary schools which are listed as feeder schools for X Academy. (specified in guidance notes)

Criteria 4

Children who do not qualify under criteria 1-3, but for whom X Academy is the nearest High School.

Criteria 5

Any other children.

Tie break

Within each criterion, if there is oversubscription, remaining places available will be allocated according to distance. Children living closest to the Academy will, therefore, be allocated a place before those who live further away. Should two or more children still be tied for a single available place, the drawing of lots will be used to decide the case.

This example is used for Case Study 3

Fair banding

Some schools use a fair banding system as part of the process of allocating places. These schools have an assessment process which determines which band each child is placed in. They then allocate places to children from each of these bands, using oversubscription criteria within the bands.

It is very important to research this type of system carefully, as they can differ between schools but if assessment is required, children who miss this (i.e. late application) will normally have a much reduced chance of a successful allocation as applications from children who did attend the assessment would usually be considered before considering applications from children who were not assessed.

Example

Students who take the fair banding assessment are considered for admission first.

Late applicants and those who do not attend the fair banding assessment will only be considered if the total number of places available are not filled by the students who attended the fair banding assessment.

Children with statements of special educational needs are admitted as a result of the academy being named in the statement and they are counted against the number of places available. They must still attend the Fair Banding Assessment. After assessment, children will be placed into one of four bands based on their assessment. 25% of the places are allocated to each of the four bands.

Places will be allocated from each band in accordance with the following oversubscription criteria:

a) Students in public care (Looked After children), previously looked after but immediately after became subject to an adoption, child arrangements, or those with a residency order or special guardianship.

b) Students whose brothers and sisters, including step-brothers and step-sisters, living at the same address, who will still be attending The X Academy at the start of the next Academic Year.

c) Children of staff employed at the Academy for a period of at least 2 years.

d) Students already educated within the same Multi-Academy Trust as The X Academy.

e) Students for whom The X Academy is the nearest school, taking into account the Local Education Authority community schools.

f) Distance from the Academy.

This example is used for Case Study 4

Catchment area

Some Local Education Authorities and Academies use the catchment area system. This gives priority to applicants from certain specified areas. If you are considering a school which has this system, it is important to find out if you are within the catchment area. Also remember that although priority will usually be given to applicants from within a catchment area, this does not always guarantee that everyone applying from within that area will be allocated a place if there is a high level of oversubscription for the school. Conversely, if you are outside the catchment area, you can still apply for a place at the school however you should remember that you would be given a lower priority when places are allocated than those applicants who are within the catchment area so if the school is oversubscribed your chances of being allocated a place will be lower than for than people who do live within the catchment area unless you qualify for another, higher oversubscription criteria within the school's admission arrangements.

It is important to clarify whether the school which you are considering does use the catchment area system. Many parents come to appeals and say that they live within the catchment area of a school, but the school in question does not use a catchment area system. The parents think that they live within the catchment area because neighbouring and nearby children attend the school but unless the oversubscription criteria state that a catchment area system is used, this is not the same thing.

Further information about why a place is not guaranteed at a school even if your neighbours' children attend the school is given in Chapter 6.

Example 1

If there are fewer applicants than there are places available, everyone who applies will be offered a place.

When there are more applicants than there are places available there has to be a way of deciding which children are offered places. This is done by having admission criteria, also known as oversubscription criteria, which are considered in order. The admission criteria for community and voluntary controlled schools are:

1. children in public care (looked after children) or a child who was previously looked after;

2. children who live in the school's Priority Admission Area (PAA) who have a brother or sister attending from the same address at the date of admission (the sibling rule);

3. children who live in the school's PAA;

4. children who live outside the school's PAA who have a brother or sister attending from the same address at the date of admission (the sibling rule);

5. children who live outside the school's PAA.

Community and controlled schools will admit a child with a Statement of Special Educational Needs where the school is named on the statement.

This example is used for Case Study 5

Example 2

This is another example of a school using catchment areas, however this one specifies an inner and outer catchment area. It also gives priority to children of staff who will have worked at the school for two years at the time of admission, and to children who are eligible for Pupil Premium because they are currently in receipt of Free School Meals (other than the usual universal Free School Meals for Reception, Year 1 and Year 2).

Process of Application for entry to Reception

a) There will be a Published Admissions Number (PAN) of 26.

b) To ensure that we are meeting the needs of parents in the local area children will be accepted from an area which will be split into a defined inner catchment area (AX -) and an outer catchment area (all other postal codes). 45% of places will be allocated to pupils in AX10 0--; AX17 8-- and AX17 9--; a further 45% of places will be allocated to AX17 5--, AX17 6--, and AX17 7--, and the final 10% of places will be allocated to pupils from the other postal code areas of AX12-7; AX16-9; IZ27-0; IZ11-1 and IZ16-3 with initial priority going to those who live1 within a two mile radius of the school.

Oversubscription criteria will be applied to the bands in each of these groups.

Oversubscription Criteria:

After children with statements of Special Educational Needs, where The School has agreed to be named on the statement, and children of members of staff who, at the time of admission, will have worked at the school for two years or more, or those employed to meet a skills shortage, the criteria will be applied in the order in which they are set out below:

a) Children in public care or adopted children who have been in public care at the date that the relevant application for admissions is made, and whom a local authority have confirmed will continue to be looked after (if still in public care) in accordance with the relevant legislation at the time they are admitted to the school.

b) Children who are eligible for the Pupil Premium because they are currently in receipt of Free School Meal Funding. (Please note this does not include the Universal Free School Meal entitlement for Key Stage 1).

c) Children who have an older sibling at the school in Years 1-11 at the time of admission.

d) Other children. The remaining places to other children will be allocated by independently scrutinised random selection to obtain a representative cohort as indicated in paragraph 1b.

Selective

Some schools (Grammar Schools) require that children that wish to apply for admission to the school do a Selection Test. The tests of all the children participating in the process are marked. The schools will often specify a certain value such as the top 25% of children in the tests will be deemed as suitable to attend the school. Once the tests have been marked and the top 25% of children identified, this allows the school to determine the "cut off" mark i.e. the mark of the last child deemed "suitable" for the selective school. Parents of all children who have participated in the test are informed if their child has attained the marks necessary to be deemed suitable. These schools are different to all other schools, as they do not have to admit up to their full Pupil Admission Number if there are not enough children who have qualified as suitable in an admission round. These schools are Selective Schools.

Once the parents of all children who have participated in the tests have been informed of the results, the parents of those deemed suitable can then add the Selective School to their preferences for their school application. The applications will then be treated as for any other school application bar the fact that only those children that have been deemed suitable would be allocated a place. If the school is oversubscribed, then the places would be allocated in accordance with the oversubscription criteria of the school as for any other school. This means that although a child could pass the tests well and be deemed suitable, if the school was oversubscribed they might not be allocated a place at the school. For any Selective School that you may be considering, contact the School for a copy of their Oversubscription Criteria and details of their testing process and key dates.

The Oversubscription Criteria for Selective Schools vary widely but the principles are the same as for the examples provided for other schools in this chapter. If you are considering a Selective Grammar School contact the School for a copy of its Oversubscription Criteria.

One very important thing to note should you be considering applying for a Selective School is that their processes can start earlier than other schools. For example they might hold their Open Evening in July (when your child is in Year 5). Parents may then need to register their child to participate for the Selection Process and the tests are often held at the start of the Autumn Term, with parents being notified of the results of the tests prior to the deadline for applications for School Places. This means if you are interested in a Selective School you must find out as early as possible the key dates so that you do not find that you have missed the deadline to register your child for the tests.

There is not a Case Study for Selective Schools because the Oversubscription Criteria can vary so much between schools, but the principle of allocating places according to the criteria in which the applicants are placed will be the same. Applicants must be determined "suitable" in order to be considered for a place. Should there not be enough eligible applicants, Selective Schools do not have to admit to the full Pupil Admission Number. If you are considering a Selective School, it is very important to contact the school for information on their particular process and Oversubscription Criteria as early as possible, probably during the start of the year in which your child is in Year 5 so that you know all of the relevant dates and deadlines.

Faith (Roman Catholic and Church of England)

Faith Schools will often give priority in their oversubscription criteria to those who follow the relevant faith for that school. Different schools have different ways of doing this. Catholic Schools tend to give priority to Baptised Catholics (and sometimes just below that, Catechumens- children who have expressed a desire and intent to become Baptised Catholics). Church of England Schools tend to prioritise according to Church attendance over a period of time, often two years. Sometimes they have additional criteria so that additional priority can be given to those that worship at the Church affiliated to that particular school above those that worship at other Churches.

Faith Schools often require the completion and submission of a Supplementary Information Form (SIF) with the school application. It is very important to find out if this is required for the school that you are considering, and if so ensure that the form is completed and submitted with the application, or directly to the school as required. These forms are where applicants can enter information relevant to their application such as church attendance or evidence of baptism. Without this information, an application would be given a much lower priority when the places are allocated, even if an applicant does fulfil the criteria as the information needs to be provided. Admission Authorities will usually then verify the information on the form prior to the process of places being allocated so that applications can be ranked in accordance with the admissions policy.

Faith Schools often give priority to applicants who fulfil their faith criteria over non faith siblings. This can lead to the situation where in years of particularly high demand, non-faith children with siblings at the school will not be offered a place because the places have all been allocated to children who have qualified under a higher priority i.e. the faith criteria. This situation causes great problems to all those involved – the families then face the situation where they would have to take their children to different schools, and it is not always possible to move the first child to another school to enable a family to have all children at the same school together. Often, the first sibling has been allocated a place at the school in years of lower demand where either the school was not oversubscribed, or they were a low priority but lived close to the school so were successful because although they came under a lower priority they were one of the first children in that category due to their proximity to the school.

Example 1- Church of England (Voluntary Aided)

Categories where all children will automatically be offered a place.

A. A child who has a statement of special educational needs which names Barnaba's CofE School.

B. Looked after children including those who were looked after but have become subject to adoption, residency or special guardianship order

C. A child or main carer has exceptional medical or mobility needs which can only be met at this school. In order to be considered under this category the application must be supported by a written recommendation from the appropriate medical professional.

In the event that there are more applications than there are places available, applications will be allocated in accordance with the following oversubscription criteria:

1. A child who has a brother or sister attending the school who will still be on the roll of the school at the expected date that the younger child is due to start (brother or sister being blood relations or adopted or fostered and living within the same household)

2. The child and parent/ guardian regularly and frequently worship(s) at Barnaba's Church

3. A child who lives within Barnaba's Parish. A map is available in school and attached to this policy

4. The child and parent/ guardian regularly and frequently worships at another Christian church which is affiliated to Churches Together in Britain and Ireland or one in full sympathy with its Trinitarian Creed

5. The child and parent/ guardian regularly and frequently attend a place of worship according to any of the following faiths: Buddhism, Hinduism, Islam, Judaism, Sikhism.

6. Any other children

This example is used for Case Study 6.

Example 2- Roman Catholic

At any time where there are more applications for places than the number of places available, places will be offered in the following order of priority:

1. Children looked after from Catholic families or children from Catholic families who were previously looked after but ceased to be so because they became adopted or became subject to a residence or special guardianship order with siblings who attend St Agatha's Catholic School.

2. Children looked after from Catholic families or children from Catholic families who were previously looked after but ceased to be so because they became adopted or became subject to a residence or special guardianship order

3. Baptised Catholic children with siblings who attend St Agatha's Catholic School

4. Baptised Catholic Children who live in the defined area.

5. Other Baptised Catholic Children.

6. Other looked after children or other children who were previously looked after but ceased to be so because they became adopted or became subject to a residence or special guardianship order with siblings who attend St Agatha's Catholic School.

7. Other looked after children or other children who were previously looked after but ceased to be so because they became adopted or became subject to a residence or special guardianship order

8. Other children with siblings who attend St Agatha's Catholic School.

9. Other children.

This example is used for Case Study 7

Schools that give priority to applicants with special aptitudes

Some schools give priority to children with special aptitude in a particular subject or sport. These schools are allowed to give priority to 10% of their total intake for special aptitude. For example if a school had a Pupil Admission Number of 300, they could give priority to 30 children under this criteria.

The School Admission Code 2014 states that "schools are restricted on the subjects on which they may select for aptitude in this way. The specialist subjects are:

a) physical education or sport, or one or more sports;

b) the performing arts, or any one or more of those arts;

c) the visual arts, or any one or more of those arts;

d) modern foreign languages, or any such language; and

e) design and technology and information technology"

If a school has chosen to give priority to children with special aptitude, it will state this in its oversubscription criteria. If the school you are considering does this, and you would like your child to be assessed you will need to find out from the school how to register them for the assessment. Schools do the assessments at different times so this is something to find out as early as possible so that you do not miss the assessments. If you feel that your child may qualify as having a special aptitude as specified by the school, and the school is a popular one that may be oversubscribed, it is well worth looking into this as if your child is granted the special aptitude criteria, their chances of gaining a place at the school would be significantly higher.

Example

Where the number of applications for admission is greater than the published admission number, applications will be considered against the criteria set out below.

a. Children in public care or fostered under an arrangement by the local authority b. 18 students (10% of the agreed admission number) will be admitted on the basis of aptitude in Performing Arts, using a specified assessment process (based on auditions) which will be set out in the published School prospectus.

c. Students whose siblings currently attend the school and who will continue to do so on the date of admission.

d. Nearest school: Students for whom X School is the nearest in a straight line, taking into account the local Community Schools.

e. Admissions of students on the basis of proximity to the school using straight line measurement from the school to the child's home.

This example is used for Case Study 8

5 CASE STUDIES

<u>Summary</u>

This chapter uses case studies to show how the examples of different types of Oversubscription Criteria in the previous chapter could work in practice. Each Oversubscription Criteria is summarised and then followed by a case study to show how applicants might be ranked under those criteria. Example applicants are listed below and the same ones will be used for each Oversubscription Criteria. This is intended to demonstrate both how the ranking process works in practice, and also how the ranking given will vary between the different sets of Oversubscription Criteria applied to the same applicants. For the sake of demonstration, it is assumed that each applicant was allowed to list enough preferences to include all of the example Oversubscription Criteria. The distances and hypothetical demand for each school will be shown for each example. The final section will then show which place each applicant would be offered based on their ranking under each Oversubscription Criteria and then the order they put their preferences in.

Notes:

None of the example applicants have been listed as coming under the Looked After or Statement of Special Educational Needs categories because these children would always be allocated a place first (as long as the necessary information is provided with the application to ensure that they are placed in this category) as this is a legal requirement.

For simplicity, it is assumed that these are all Secondary Schools as this will allow a better illustration of the effect of the different criteria on the ranking of applicants and which places are finally offered to the applicants. The mechanism of Oversubscription Criteria to rank applicants, and the way that the final school offered is determined is the same for both Secondary and Primary Schools.

Example applicants:

- Rosemary – has an older sibling at Secondary School who will be going into Year 12.
- George- Is a Baptised Catholic
- Angela- Goes to Church regularly
- James- has an older sibling at Secondary who will be going into Year 9.
- Catherine- is an oldest child. She loves Drama and has been studying this for a few years now.

Case Study 1 – Standard Local Education Authority

The priorities and their order in the Oversubscription Criteria are summarised in the table below:

Priority 1	Looked after children and children with Special Education Needs or exceptional medical or mobility needs that can only be met at that specific school
Priority 2	Children with older brothers or sisters who will still be at the school at the start of the next academic year (i.e. when the applicant starts school)
Priority 3	Children who attend a linked (feeder) school
Priority 4	Children for whom it is their nearest school
Priority 5	All other children

This school has a Pupil Admission Number (PAN) of 180.

Total preferences made: 212

The preferences were placed into the criteria as shown below:

Priority 1 – 7

Priority 2 - 45

Priority 3- 39

Priority 4- 57

<u>Priority 5 - 64</u>

Total- 212

All the children in Priorities 1-4 were allocated a place, taking 148 places.

Priority 5- the first 32 children in this Priority group would have been offered a place after the initial ranking, taking the total places allocated to 180 places (the PAN). The children were ranked within this criteria on distance from the school. The cut off distance (distance that the last child offered a place lived from the school) was 2.72 miles.

	Priority under Oversubscription Criteria	Distance from school	Successful in ranking?
Rosemary	5	2.39 miles	Yes
George	5	3.40 miles	No
Angela	3- Angela attends a feeder school	4.26 miles	Yes
James	5	1.90 miles	Yes
Catherine	4- this is Catherine's nearest school	1.10 miles	Yes

All the applicants except for James would have been offered a place in this scenario. James was not successful because he came under Priority 5 (All other children) but he lived 3.40 miles away from the school, the last child offered a place under that Priority lived 2.72 miles away.

Case Study 2- Academy (1)

The priorities and their order in the Oversubscription Criteria are summarised in the table below:

Priority 1	Looked after children and previously looked after children
Priority 2	Children with exceptional medical or mobility needs which can only be met by this Academy
Priority 3	Children with brothers or sisters who will be at the Academy at the start of the next academic year
Priority 4	Children for whom the Academy is their nearest school
Priority 5	All other children

This school has a Pupil Admission Number (PAN) of 150

Total preferences made: 179

The preferences were placed into the criteria as shown below:

>Priority 1 – 2
>
>Priority 2 - 3
>
>Priority 3- 51
>
>Priority 4- 27
>
>Priority 5 - 96
>
>**Total- 179**

All the children in Priorities 1-4 were allocated a place, taking 83 places.

Priority 5- the first 67 children in this Priority group would have been successful in the ranking process. The cut off distance for Priority 5 was 1.89 miles. 29 children were unsuccessful.

	Priority under Oversubscription Criteria	Distance from school	Successful in ranking?
Rosemary	5	2.79 miles	No
George	5	1.78 miles	Yes
Angela	4- this is Angela's nearest school	1.02 miles	Yes
James	4- this is James' nearest school	0.56 miles	Yes
Catherine	5	2.37 miles	No

George, Angela and James qualified for places at this school. It was the nearest school for James and Angela so they came into the higher oversubscription criteria for this. Rosemary and Catherine were unsuccessful as they lived out with the cut off distance.

Case Study 3 – Academy (2)

The priorities and their order in the Oversubscription Criteria are summarised in the table below:

Priority 1	Children who are or have been in public care or fostered under an arrangement made by the Local Authority and children who have special educational / medical / mobility needs which can only be met by this Academy
Priority 2	Children with older brothers or sisters(who live in the same house as the applicant) who will be on roll in Years 7-11 at the Academy at the start of the next academic year
Priority 3	Children who attend a linked (feeder) school
Priority 4	Children for whom it is their nearest school
Priority 5	All other children

This school has a Pupil Admission Number (PAN) of 240

Total preferences made: 479

The preferences were placed into the criteria as shown below:

Priority 1 – 5

Priority 2 - 89

Priority 3- 47

Priority 4- 74

Priority 5 - 264

Total- 479

This Academy was very oversubscribed, with 479 preferences for 240 places.

All the children in Priorities 1-4 were successful in the ranking. The first 25 children in Priority 5 were successful.

The cut off distance for Priority 5 was 1.21 miles. The cut off distance for Priority 4 (nearest school) was 3.07 miles. Sometimes children whose nearest school can live further away than the last child in for whom it wasn't their nearest school.

	Priority under Oversubscription Criteria	Distance from school	Successful in ranking?
Rosemary	5- Rosemary's older sibling attends this school but will be in Year 12 at the start of the next academic year. This Academy gives sibling priority to those applicants who have a sibling who will be in Years 7-11 at the start of the next academic year. Rosemary didn't qualify for sibling priority.	1.46 miles	No
George	4- this is George's nearest school	0.79 miles	Yes
Angela	5	1.86 miles	No
James	2- James' sibling attends this school and will be in Year 9 at the start of the next academic year. This means that James was granted sibling priority in the oversubscription criteria.	3.67 miles	Yes
Catherine	5	1.43 miles	No

James qualified for a place at this school. Although at 3.67 miles away, he was well outside the cut off distance, he has a sibling who would still be at school in Year 9 when he is due to start school so he qualified for the sibling priority. George qualified for a place as he lived very close to the school and it was his nearest school so he came under the nearest school criteria. Rosemary didn't qualify for a place at the school, although she has a sibling who will be attending the school, they will not be in a qualifying year group so she was not granted sibling priority. She was placed in Priority 5 but lived out with the cut off distance for the school. Angela and Catherine didn't get places at the school as they lived out with the cut off distance for the school under Priority 5 as it wasn't their nearest school.

Case Study 4 – Fair Banding

The priorities and their order in the Oversubscription Criteria are summarised in the table below:

Students who take the fair banding assessment will be considered for admission first. Late applicants and those who do not attend the fair banding assessment will only be considered if the total number of places available are not filled by the students who attended the fair banding assessment. Children with statements of special educational needs are admitted as a result of the academy being named in the statement and they are counted against the number of places available. They must still attend the Fair Banding Assessment. After assessment, children will be placed into one of the four bands based on their assessment. 25% of the places are allocated to each of the four bands.

Priority 1	Looked after children, children previously looked after but immediately afterwards became subject to an adoption, child arrangements or those with a residency order or special guardianship
Priority 2	Children with siblings (including step siblings) living at the same address who will be on roll at the school at the start of the next academic year
Priority 3	Children of staff employed at the school for at least two years at the time of application
Priority 4	Children already educated within the same Multi-Academy Trust as the school
Priority 5	Children for whom the school is their nearest school (taking into account Local Education Community Schools)
Priority 6	Distance from the Academy

This school has a Pupil Admission Number (PAN) of 120.

Total preferences made: 119 – Out of these, 112 attended for Fair Banding

The preferences were placed into the criteria as shown below.

	Band 1	Band 2	Band 3	Band 4	Total
Priority 1	1	0	2	0	3
Priority 2	7	4	6	9	26
Priority 3	0	2	1	0	3
Priority 4	4	12	5	4	25
Priority 5	6	7	7	3	23
Priority 6	5	3	9	5	22
Total	*23*	*28*	*30*	*21*	*102*
Didn't attend Fair Banding	7				
Total places offered	**119**				

This school was undersubscribed. The table above shows how the applications were ranked in the oversubscription criteria. Because there were less applications than places, all applicants were offered a place. If the school had been oversubscribed by more applicants who had not attended the fair banding, they would have been ranked according to the oversubscription criteria in order to determine which of them would have been offered the remaining places.

If there had been 120 or more applicants who had attended the Fair Banding assessment, the places would have been offered to the applicants who attended the Fair Banding assessment after they had been ranked according to the oversubscription criteria and not to those who had not attended, even if they had siblings at the school or it was their nearest school as those applicants who had been assessed for Fair Banding would be considered first as stated in the Admission Arrangements.

	Priority under Oversubscription Criteria	Distance from school	Successful in ranking?
Rosemary	6- Band 2	2.45 miles	Yes
George	6- Band 1	1.02 miles	Yes
Angela	Didn't attend Fair Banding	3.96 miles	Yes
James	6- Band 4	0.79 miles	Yes
Catherine	Didn't attend Fair Banding	1.76 miles	Yes

Because the school was undersubscribed, all children qualified for a place at the school.

Case Study 5- Catchment Area

The priorities and their order in the Oversubscription Criteria are summarised in the table below:

Where there is more than one child in one Priority, their distance from the school will be used to rank them with nearest first.

Priority 1	Looked after and previously looked after children
Priority 2	Children from the school's Priority Admission Area who have a brother or sister living at the same address who will be attending the school at the date of admission
Priority 3	Children who live in the school's Priority Admission Area
Priority 4	Children who live outside the school's Priority Admission Area who have a brother or sister living at the same address who will be attending the school at the date of admission
Priority 5	Children who live outside the school's Priority Admission Area

This school has a Pupil Admission Number (PAN) of 300

Total preferences made: 410

The preferences were placed into the criteria as shown below:

Priority 1 – 9

Priority 2 - 68

Priority 3- 179

Priority 4- 42

Priority 5 - 112

Total- 410

All applicants in Priorities 1-4 were successful in the ranking for places. The first 2 applicants in Priority 5 were allocated a place, with 110 applicants being unsuccessful. The cut off distance for the school in Priority 5- the distance for the last child offered a place was 2.69 miles.

	Priority under Oversubscription Criteria	Distance from school	Successful in ranking?
Rosemary	3- Lives in the Priority Admission area	1.06 miles	Yes
George	5	2.85 miles	No
Angela	5	4.68 miles	No
James	5	3.07 miles	No
Catherine	3- Lives in the Priority Admission Area	0.76 miles	Yes

Rosemary and Catherine both qualified for a place at this school as they live within the catchment area (Criteria 3). The other children did not qualify for a place as they all live out with the cut off distance and came under Criteria 5.

Case Study 6- Faith School- Church of England

Categories where all children will automatically be offered a place.
A. A child who has a statement of special educational needs which names Barnaba's CofE School.
B. Looked after children including those who were looked after but have become subject to adoption, residency or special guardianship order
C. A child or main carer has exceptional medical or mobility needs which can only be met at this school. In order to be considered under this category the application must be supported by a written recommendation from the appropriate medical professional.

In the event that there are more applications than there are places available, applications will be allocated in accordance with the following oversubscription criteria:

The priorities and their order in the Oversubscription Criteria are summarised in the following table:

Priority 1	A child who has a brother or sister attending the school who will still be on the roll of the school at the expected date that the younger child is due to start (brother or sister being blood relations or adopted or fostered and living within the same household)
Priority 2	The child and parent/ guardian regularly and frequently worship(s) at Barnaba's Church
Priority 3	A child who lives within Barnaba's Parish. A map is available in school and attached to this policy
Priority 4	The child and parent/ guardian regularly and frequently worships at another Christian church which is affiliated to Churches Together in Britain and Ireland or one in full sympathy with its Trinitarian Creed
Priority 5	The child and parent/ guardian regularly and frequently attend a place of worship according to any of the following faiths: Buddhism, Hinduism, Islam, Judaism, Sikhism.
Priority 6	Any other children

This school has a Pupil Admission Number (PAN) of 150

Total preferences made: 177

6 places were allocated to applicants who came under Categories A, B and C. The other applications were placed into the Oversubscription Criteria as shown below:

Priority 1 – 69

Priority 2 - 30

Priority 3- 17

Priority 4- 22

Priority 5 – 22

Priority 6- 33

Total- 177

All applicants in Priorities 1-5 qualified for a place under the Oversubscription Criteria. The first 6 applicants in Priority 6 qualified for a place, with the cut off distance being 1.35 miles.

	Priority under Oversubscription Criteria	Distance from school	Successful in ranking?
Rosemary	3- Lives in Barnabas Parish	0.65 miles	Yes
George	6	1.98 miles	No
Angela	2- Angela regularly goes to St Barnaba's Church and provided proof of this so that she was placed into Priority 2	2.79 miles	Yes
James	6	1.54 miles	No
Catherine	6	2.32 miles	No

Angela qualified for a place at the school as she was a regular church goer and had provided the necessary information for this to be verified and her be placed into Criteria 2. Rosemary qualified for Criteria 3 as she lives within the Parish. George, James and Catherine were all placed into Criteria 6 and lived outside the cut off distance so did not qualify for a place at the school.

Case Study 7- Faith School- Roman Catholic

Priority 1	Looked after or previously looked after children from Catholic families with siblings at St Agatha's Catholic School
Priority 2	Looked after or previously looked after children from Catholic families
Priority 3	Baptised Catholic children with siblings who attend St Agatha's Catholic School
Priority 4	Baptised Catholic children who live within the defined area
Priority 5	Other Baptised Catholic children
Priority 6	Other looked after or previously looked after children with siblings who attend St Agatha's Catholic School
Priority 7	Other looked after or previously looked after children
Priority 8	Other children with siblings who attend St Agatha's Catholic School
Priority 9	Other children

This school has a Pupil Admission Number (PAN) of 175.
Total preferences made: 207
The preferences were placed into the criteria as shown below:

Priority 1 – 2

Priority 2 - 1

Priority 3- 53

Priority 4- 47

Priority 5 – 62

Priority 6- 0

Priority 7- 1

Priority 8- 16

Priority 9- 27

Total- 207

All the children in Priorities 1-7 were successful and would have been allocated places in the ranking. The applicants in Priority 8 (Other children with siblings who attend the school) were ranked by distance, and the first 9 would have been allocated places were allocated places with a cut off distance of 2.06 miles. This meant that the other 5 applicants in that Priority were unsuccessful. No applicants from Priority 9 (Other children) were successful as all the places had been allocated before reaching that Priority.

	Priority under Oversubscription Criteria	Distance from school	Successful in ranking?
Rosemary	9	1.69 miles	No
George	5- Baptised Catholic

George lives further away than the cut off distance, but he would have been offered a place because he is in a higher category than the children where the cut off applied (Other children with siblings) | 3.20 miles | Yes |
Angela	9	0.75 miles	No
James	9	1.69 miles	No
Catherine	9	1.20 miles	No

George lives outside the cut off distance but was placed into Priority 5 (Baptised Catholic) and therefore qualified for a place at the school. All the other children were placed into Priority 9- no applicants from this priority were successful so they did not qualify for a place at the school.

Case Study 8- Special Aptitudes

Priority 1	Children in public care or fostered under an arrangement with the Local Authority
Priority 2	18 students (10% of the agreed admission number) will be admitted on the basis of aptitude in Performing Arts using a specified assessment process (based on auditions) which will be set out in the published School prospectus
Priority 3	Children whose siblings currently attend the school and who will continue to do so on the date of admission
Priority 4	Students for whom the School is their nearest in a straight line, taking into account local Community Schools
Priority 5	Admission of students on the basis of proximity to the school using straight line measurement from the school to the child's home

This school has a Pupil Admission Number (PAN) of 180.

Total preferences made: 202

The preferences were placed into the criteria as shown below:

Priority 1 – 7

Priority 2 - 18

Priority 3- 56

Priority 4- 32

Priority 5 - 89

Total- 202

Children who applied for the Special Aptitude Priority auditioned, and 18 qualified for this criteria. All applicants from Priorities 1-4 were successful in being ranked for a place. Applicants from Priority 5 were ranked by distance and 67 were allocated places, with a cut off distance of 3.17 miles. 22 applicants from Priority 5 were unsuccessful.

	Priority under Oversubscription Criteria	Distance from school	Successful at ranking?
Rosemary	5	4.02 miles	No
George	5	3.20 miles	No
Angela	5	3.75 miles	No
James	5	4.19 miles	No
Catherine	2- Granted Priority 2 after assessment at audition Catherine lives well beyond the cut off distance for the school, but is successful in the ranking because she was placed in Priority 2- Special Aptitude following a successful assessment process.	4.67 miles	Yes

Catherine successfully auditioned and was placed in Priority 2 so qualified for a place at the school even though she lives 4.67 miles away so well outside the cut off distances. All the other children were placed into Priority 5 and also lived outside the cut off distance so they didn't qualify for a place at the school.

Final Allocation of Places

The Case Studies above demonstrate how the oversubscription criteria are used to rank applicants, and how applicants are placed into the different Criteria in order to determine which applicants would qualify to be offered a place at a school.

Because applicants are allowed to make more than one preference, the Local Authority coordinates all preferences and ensures that if an applicant is successfully ranked in more than one of their preferences, the school they are offered is at the highest preference for which they could be offered a place. This is why it is important to consider the order in which you list the schools that you are preferencing.

The following table gives details of each of the example children used in the Case Studies- their order of preferences and the final school place that they would be offered on National Offer Day. More details about each example child's application and final allocation.

Preference	Child / Preference / Qualified for Place?				
	Rosemary	George	Angela	James	Catherine
1	Academy 2 - No	Roman Catholic School - Yes	Church of England School – Yes	Academy 2 - Yes	Academy 2 - No
2	Academy 1 - Yes	Special Aptitude School – No	Special Aptitude School - No	Special Aptitude School - No	Academy 1 - No
3	Local Education Authority - Yes	Academy 2 - Yes	Local Education Authority - Yes	Catchment Area School - No	Special Aptitude School – Yes
4	Catchment Area School - Yes	Academy 1 - Yes	Academy 2 - No	Local Education Authority – Yes	Catchment Area School - Yes
5	Church of England School - Yes	Local Education Authority - No	Academy 1 - Yes	Academy 1 - Yes	Local Education Authority - Yes
6	Roman Catholic School - No	Fair Banding School – Yes	Fair Banding School – Yes	Church of England School - No	Fair Banding School - No
7	Fair Banding School - Yes	Church of England School - No	Catchment Area School – No	Roman Catholic School - No	Roman Catholic School - No
8	Special Aptitude School - No	Catchment Area School - No	Roman Catholic School - No	Fair Banding School - Yes	Church of England School - No
School Place offered at:	Academy 1	Roman Catholic School	Church of England School	Academy 2	Special Aptitude School

Rosemary
Rosemary's first preference was Academy 2, where she had a sibling who would be going into Year 12. Because the Oversubscription Criteria for this school only let applicants qualify for sibling priority if their siblings were between Years 7-11 at the time of entry, she did not get sibling priority. This meant that she was unsuccessful as she lived further than the cut off distance.

Rosemary's highest preference school where she was successful in ranking was Academy 1. Therefore this is where she was offered a place.

George
George was offered his first preference school, the Roman Catholic School. Although he lived quite far from the school, because he was a Baptised Catholic he was placed into a higher priority within the Oversubscription Criteria which meant that he qualified for a place.

Angela
Angela was offered a place at her first preference, the Church of England School. Although she lived well beyond the final cut off distance, because she was a regular attender at the Church named in the Oversubscription Criteria, and had provided proof of this with her application, she was placed in the higher Priority and therefore was successful in obtaining a place at the school.

James
James was offered a place at his first preference, Academy 2. Although he lived far beyond the cut off distance, because he had a sibling who would be going into Year 9 he qualified for sibling priority.

Catherine
Catherine did not qualify for a place at her first or second preference schools. She was offered a place at her third preference, the Special Aptitude School. This was because she had successfully auditioned which had qualified her to be placed into the Special Aptitude Priority. Had she not qualified for this, she would not have been offered a place as she lived far beyond the cut off distance for the school.

6 COMMON ASSUMPTIONS MADE BY PARENTS

<u>Summary</u>

Sometimes parents assume that their child will be allocated a place at the school they want if they apply for it. Unfortunately this is not always the case. Often when these parents come to appeal, they mention why they thought they would get a place at the school. This chapter lists some of the assumptions most commonly made by parents and explains why they are not always correct. By explaining why they can be incorrect, it is hoped that readers will avoid making these mistakes and improve their chances of a successful school application. They will have a better understanding of how the system of allocating school places works and what they should research before they apply for school places.

The key message from this chapter is that parents should research the oversubscription criteria for the schools they are considering. This should prevent many of the assumptions listed being made which could result in parents preferencing schools which they are then unsuccessful for, and the stress and worry this causes while they try to secure a place at a school they would be happy with.

If you understand all these after you have read this chapter that will help you when you come to research schools and their oversubscription criteria when you are deciding which schools to put on your application.

The Local Education Authority will write to me to tell me when I need to apply

This is maybe the most fundamental assumption that some parents make- they assume that they will get a letter to tell them when to apply for a school place. There is no statutory requirement for Local Education Authorities to write to parents to inform them of this. Some Local Education Authorities do try to write to parents, but it is an impossible task to write to all families as there are always some people who have moved and not redirected their mail. Efforts are usually made to try to reach parents to remind them to apply for a school place in other ways, such as putting up posters in nurseries, community centres, libraries etc. But there is no legal requirement for Local Education Authorities to write to notify parents of the need to apply for a place for their child, the onus is definitely on parents to find out when they need to do this and then apply within the required timescales.

Catchment areas

Many parents will say that they don't understand why their child didn't get a place at a school "because they live in the catchment area". This is probably the most commonly made assumption that I encounter at Appeal Hearings. The schools in question when this is said usually don't use the catchment area system in their allocation process.

The parents assume that they live in the catchment area because they see local children, even children living in the same street, who are attending the school. They are right that children from their area are attending the school but this is not the same thing as living within a school's catchment area.

The chapters on Oversubscription Criteria show that Catchment areas are used in the oversubscription criteria of some, but not all, schools. For those schools who do operate a catchment area system, children living within defined catchment areas are given a higher priority in the oversubscription criteria. If you think a school you are considering uses a catchment area system, it is important to check this out by finding the school's Admission Arrangements which will include their Oversubscription Criteria. This will tell you if the school does use a catchment area system. If it does, you will be able to find out either from the school or the Local Education Authority whether you are in their catchment area.

If the school operates a catchment area system, and you are within it, this is good news as it does increase your chance of being offered a place at the school depending on how high the catchment area priority is placed within the school's oversubscription criteria. Remember though, living in catchment area does not guarantee getting a place at a school. It means your application would be ranked higher amongst the applications but getting a place would depend on how many other applications there were and how many were ranked above and below yours. It is possible depending on where catchment is placed in the oversubscription criteria for not all applicants in this category to be offered a place should there be a high level of demand and large numbers of other applicants being ranked in a higher category. It is a good idea to find out from the Local Education Authority levels of demand in previous years and if the school was oversubscribed the distance and criteria of the last child offered a place in those previous years. You will not be able to predict what would happen in future years based on this because demand does change from year to year but it is useful to have an idea of demand in previous years.

Think about things that might have changed the level of demand for any of the schools you are considering. Examples of reasons for changes in demand for a school are:

-A school obtaining an Outstanding Ofsted rating can massively increase demand for that school, but can also decrease demand for neighbouring schools as more parents try to get places at the newly Outstanding school. Conversely, a school getting a lower Ofsted rating than it had before can reduce demand for that school.

- Exam results- if a school has an impressive improvement in its exam results this can have a dramatic effect on demand for the school. Again, a decline in exam success for a school can reduce demand for a school.

- A large housing development near to a school can reduce the cut off distance if the school gets a large number of applications from it as it would mean more places would have been used up before getting to children who lived further away (just going on distance alone without considering other oversubscription criteria used by the school)

- A popular Secondary School changing its oversubscription criteria to give priority to children who attend a certain primary school can massively increase demand for that primary school as parents try to plan for the future when their child is starting Secondary School. This can reduce demand to neighbouring primary schools who are not listed as a feeder school for the Secondary School as more parents try to get their children into the school that gives them priority for the Secondary School later on.

Neighbour's children go to the school

Often parents assume (not unreasonably) that if their neighbour's children go to the school in question, their child will get a place at the school. Unfortunately, although this is often the case, there are times when this doesn't happen.

The main reason for this is that demand can change between years. So the neighbouring child might have applied in a year when demand was low. This would mean that the school would have given places to children who were ranked further down according to the oversubscription criteria. Put simply, if less children apply, places could go to children who live further away. If lots of children apply, the places would be allocated to children living closer by and the ones living further away wouldn't be offered a place as all the places would be allocated before they were reached in the ranked list (when distance is used to rank applications).

If a school is high demand, and has been for a few years, it is still possible for children from further away who got a place at the school years before in a low demand year to affect future allocations. This could happen if the first child had a younger sibling who then applied in a later, higher demand year and gained a place because they had qualified for sibling priority under the oversubscription criteria. This could mean a child who wouldn't get in as a first child because they lived too far from the school would be allocated a place due to the sibling priority. If this was a neighbour's child, you might not know that they had had an older sibling at the school as they could have grown up and left home. Just seeing the child going to that school might mean you would assume that children from your street would get a place at the school without understanding the reasons behind why that particular child got a place or the current level of demand at the school.

This demonstrates why it is so important to research oversubscription criteria and level of demand for every school which you are considering.

Children living further away go to the school

Parents quite often come to Appeal and give details of children who live further away that have been allocated a place at the school. They understand about the relevance of distance from the school so assume that if a child who lives further away from the school has got a place, they should also have been allocated a place. If the child they mention as an example got into the school in a previous year, this can often be explained by that child's year of allocation being a low demand year.

The other explanation for this, which is more relevant when the parents are mentioning a child that was given a place in the same admission round as their unsuccessful application for the school, is that the other child might have qualified for the school under a higher Oversubscription Criteria. When this hasn't happened because of the sibling criteria, it can be because the child has been given priority because the school in question is their nearest school and priority is given for this in the school's oversubscription criteria. It is possible for a child living further away to be allocated a place because the school is their nearest school, whereas a child living closer to the school (in a different direction) could have another school as their nearest school. This would place them in a lower criteria and the places could have all been allocated to children who were ranked above them according to the oversubscription criteria. This situation would of course only occur if the school gave priority to children for whom it was their nearest school, again this can be found by reading the oversubscription criteria for the school.

The diagram demonstrates how giving children for whom it is their nearest school priority in the oversubscription criteria can mean a child living further away can be allocated a place at a school when a child living nearer doesn't get a place.

Cut off Distances for Nearest and Not Nearest School Criteria

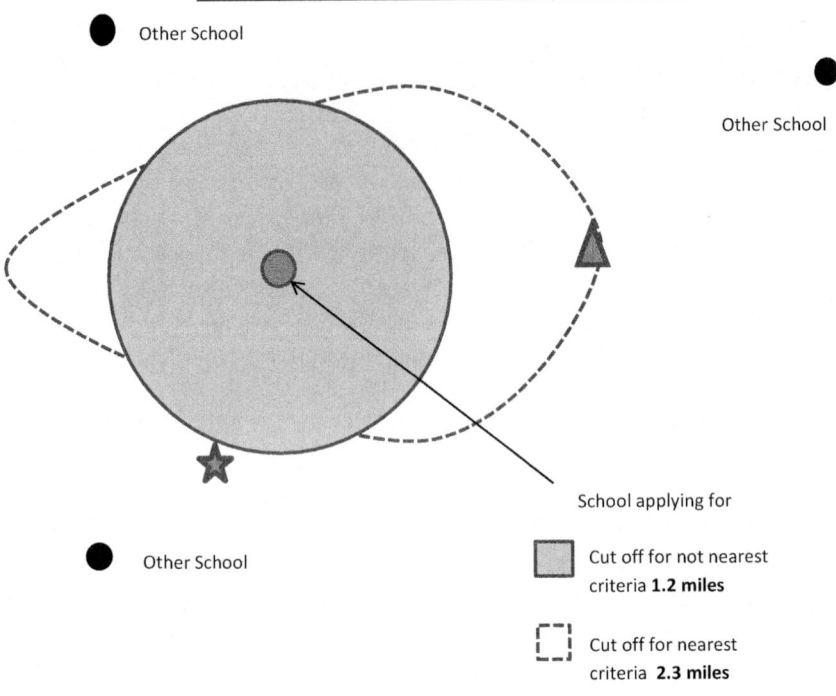

- Other School
- Other School
- School applying for
- Cut off for not nearest criteria **1.2 miles**
- Cut off for nearest criteria **2.3 miles**
- Other School

▲ Child living at this address is offered a place at the school. They live 2.3 miles away from the school but it is their nearest school.

★ Child living at this address lives just outside the cut off distance of 1.2 miles. Although they live closer to the school than the other child, it is not their nearest school. This puts them lower down when the applications are ranked under the Oversubscription Criteria and places were all allocated before their application was reached in the ranked list.

Child has an older sibling at the school

Parents can often assume that because they already have a child attending the school, this means that their younger child will be allocated a place because of sibling priority. Whilst this is true in many cases, there are instances when this doesn't happen.

One reason a child with a sibling already at the school might not get a place at the school is if they have not qualified for sibling priority. This can happen if the school specifies in their oversubscription criteria that the existing sibling at the school has to be in certain year groups. This happens with secondary schools who sometimes only give sibling priority for siblings up to a certain year group, often before the children go into Sixth Form at the School. Other secondary schools will sometimes not specify that the sibling has to be in a certain year group, but will state that sibling priority would not be given to children whose older sibling joined Sixth Form from another school.

Obviously assuming that your child will get a place at a school due to sibling priority can have devastating consequences if it turns out that this is not the case. Making this assumption could mean that parents do not fully research other schools, or only put down one preference- the one that they thought their child would get into automatically. Not getting a place at the preferred school when no other preferences were made could mean the child being allocated a place at a school that the parents hadn't even considered when had they preferenced other schools they would have had a chance at being offered a place at one of these.

The other common reason that a child with a sibling at the school doesn't get a place when they apply is in faith schools. Catholic schools in particular often have extensive lists of oversubscription criteria, and often non Catholic children, even those with siblings at the school, can be placed far down the list of oversubscription criteria below Catholic children or those living in catchment area. This means that as in the example given above, in years of low demand a child who comes into a low criteria such as a non-Catholic child living out of catchment area, could be allocated a place at the school.

However if a sibling applies in a subsequent year of high demand, it is possible that they would not get a place at the school due to being placed lower in the oversubscription criteria than children who for example are Catholic / children who are Catholic who have siblings at the school / live in the catchment area.

Both the examples above show the importance of making sure you read and understand how the oversubscription criteria at any school you are considering work so that you know how the places are allocated for the school. If you find out that your child won't get sibling priority, this is obviously going to be very disappointing, but better to find out before you apply so you can add other schools to your application as a fall-back position rather than only find out once you have had your letter to say that your child has been allocated a place at a school you have never heard of.

Moving house

Parents assume that moving house to be closer to the school they want will mean that their child will get a place at the school. Whilst this is true in some cases, it is more complicated than that.

If a parent was considering moving house to be closer to their preferred school, they would be wise to check the oversubscription criteria for the school to find out the criteria used by the school. Living in the catchment area, particularly in small primary schools, does not unfortunately always guarantee a place at the school. If there was a year with lots of children with siblings (if given priority in the oversubscription criteria), and a looked after child and a child with a Statement of Educational Needs naming the school, that could take up quite a few of the available places if the school only had a Pupil Admission Number of 30 or less.

Another thing to consider would be how popular the school is. Finding out the level of demand in previous years, and if considering moving house, the cut off distance (the distance the last child allocated a place lived from the school) would be essential information before planning a house move. Even if moving very close to the school, this would only ever improve a child's chances of getting a place, it wouldn't be possible to say for sure that an application would be successful for the reasons already given above.

If, after researching the oversubscription criteria and the previous demand, a parent still wanted to proceed with moving house near to the school, they would then have to make sure that they had moved into the new address before the closing date for applications. Local Education Authorities will always allocate places based on the current address- this is used to determine if a child lives in the catchment area and to calculate the child's distance from the schools that are preferred on their application. An address would only be changed once sufficient proof had been provided, such as a Council Tax bill, tenancy agreement, final utility bill. If a move had taken place just after the closing date, it would be up to the applicant to check with the Local Education Authority if they would change the address before the allocation process happened. Different Local Education Authorities have different processes so a parent would have to check with their Local Education Authority for advice. If a parent is intent on moving, it would be safer in terms of their application to ensure that their move was complete, and their new address accepted by the Local Education Authority prior to the closing date for peace of mind.

The only exception to Local Authorities only allocating for a new address once the move has been completed and verified is for Children of UK service personnel (UK Armed Forces). The School Admissions Code 2014 states that "for families of service personnel with a confirmed posting to their area, or crown servants returning from overseas to live in that area, admission authorities must:

a). allocate a place in advance of the family arriving in the area provided that the application is accompanied by an official letter that declares a relocation date and a Unit postal address or quartering area address when considering the application against their oversubscription criteria. This must include accepting a unit postal address or quartering area address for a service child. Admission authorities must not refuse a service child a place because the family does not currently live in the area, or reserve blocks of places for these children; and

b). ensure that arrangements in their area support the Government's commitment to removing disadvantage for service children. Arrangements must be appropriate for the area and be described in the local authority's composite prospectus"

Parents moving house after the allocation has been done are often disappointed because they assume that because they have moved into a new area, they will get a place at the school. This is often not the case. Once the places have been allocated and offered to applicants, unless the school is undersubscribed or any places are refused, there would be no places left for people coming into the area. If it is a secondary school, then there is scope for parents to appeal, but if it is a primary school where Class Size Legislation would apply to the appeal then the chances of being successful are very limited.

Anyone considering moving into a new area to secure a place at a school should research very carefully before making the final decision to move, and should remember that they are not guaranteed a place at the school they want even if they do move. Unless the move can be done before the closing date for applications in the normal admission, the chances of success are reduced so timing is another important consideration when making this decision. Living closer to the school would help with the position on the waiting list, but there is no guarantee that a place would become available.

Child attends the School's Nursery

Occasionally parents don't realise that they have to apply for a place and think that they would get a place automatically. This is not the case, and all parents have to submit an application for their child to be allocated a place at school.

Parents applying for Reception for their child sometimes assume that their child will get a place because they attend the school's Nursery setting. Although Admission Authorities are allowed to give priority to children who attend the school nursery class or school-run nursery in their oversubscription criteria, it is not compulsory and many Admission Authorities do not include this in their oversubscription criteria. It is very important to find out if this applies to the school that you are considering if your child attends their Nursery and you think they will get priority for this.

The other issue with assuming your child will get a place at a school because they attend its nursery is the number of applicants there might be for places at the school. It is easy to assume that if your child is one of 30 who attend the Nursery sessions, and there is a PAN of 30, that your child will get a place. But if the Nursery runs a morning session and an afternoon session- both with 30 children then that is 60 children attending the Nursery who might want to apply. Also remember that there may be other parents living close to the school who for whatever reason do not send their children to that Nursery- perhaps they send their child to a private setting, or they have chosen not to send their child to Nursery, or there might be other children who have sibling or other priorities under the oversubscription criteria for the school. All these reasons can mean that not all the children who attend the School's Nursery setting would be allocated a place if they all applied for a place at the school.

The School Admissions Code 2014 allows Admission Authorities to "give priority in their oversubscription criteria to children who are eligible for the early years pupil premium, the pupil premium or the service premium who:

a) are in a nursery class which is part of the school; or

b) attend a nursery that is established and run by the school. The nursery must be named in the admission arrangements and its selection must be transparent and on reasonable grounds"

If this is the case for the school that you are considering, it will state this in the school's oversubscription criteria.

Just putting one school on the application

Some parents think that if they put just one school on the application (or naming the same school as each preference), that will mean that they will get a place on at the school. This is definitely not the case. All applications for a school are ranked using the oversubscription criteria in order to determine which children would be offered a place. Only listing one school means running a real risk that the child is allocated a place at a school miles away. This is because if a child is unsuccessful in getting a place at any of the schools listed on their application, the Local Education Authority would allocate them a place at a school with places left after everyone who asked for places at schools has been accommodated. This is usually the nearest school with places, but can still be quite some distance away and often not a school that a parent would have considered or be happy with.

Putting just one preference shows our commitment to the school

Some parents believe that by putting one preference on their application, they are somehow showing commitment to the school and this will enhance their chances of getting a place at a school. I have even heard of a head teacher advising parents to do this and saying it would strengthen the parents' case should they need to go to appeal. This is just not true. Schools which are their own Admission Authorities who rank the applications themselves (before passing the ranked list back to the Local Education Authority) are never told how many preferences a parent has made on the form, or which preference their school was on 1any application. They are just given a list of names and the details needed in order to rank them according to the oversubscription criteria.

Putting just one preference out of "commitment to the school" would not, in itself, sway an Appeal Panel into granting a place. Out of all parents I have seen who have appealed after only making one preference, the vast majority were unsuccessful at appeal. Those that were successful would have had other compelling reasons to convince the panel that the child needed to go to that school.

The law gives parents the right to list at least three preferences in their application (some Local Education Authorities allow more) and it makes sense to use each of the preferences possible in order to maximise the chance of securing a place at a school which you would be happy with.

If I don't get the school that I asked for, I will be given a place at my local school

This isn't always the case. You should always put the local school down as a preference, even if it is your last preference. This means that should you be unsuccessful in getting a place at higher preferenced schools, you have a good chance of getting a place at your local school. You would have a good chance at the local school because of the reduced distance to the school (as it is your local one) and if priority is given to children for whom it is their nearest school in their oversubscription criteria this greatly improves your chance of a securing a place there.

If you don't preference the local school, there is a risk that it might fill up with children who did apply for it. If an applicant is unsuccessful in all of their preferences, the Local Education Authority will offer them a place at a school that still has spaces. Generally, Local Education Authorities will offer a place in this situation at the nearest school to the applicant that still has places available after all those that applied for schools have been allocated them. For example, if a school has a PAN of 120, and 100 places are allocated to children who have applied then it would have 20 places left. These could then be allocated to children who were unsuccessful in all of their preferences. The problem with this is that a school with places left after the initial allocation might be some distance away, if the local school has filled up with people who asked for it then there will be no places left for those who didn't put it down as a preference. Of course if the local school does have some spaces left after the initial allocation then people local to it who were unsuccessful in the preferences they put down would have a good chance of getting a place at the school but this is not guaranteed. This is why I always advise putting the local school as a preference, even as the last one to maximise the chance of getting a place there if not at higher preferenced schools because if this isn't done there is a risk that a place could be offered at a school miles away.

First Preference First

Sometimes parents think that they would get additional priority for putting a school down as their first preference. This is not the case, the School Admissions Code states that Admission Authorities are not allowed to give priority for putting a school as a first preference- termed "first preference first".

Local Education Authorities will try to allocate applicants with their highest preferenced school that they have qualified for a place at under the oversubscription criteria. If an applicant would be able to get a place at their first preference school, then they would be allocated a place at that school. But the applicant would have been allocated the place at the school because they were successful when ranked under the oversubscription criteria for the school, not because they placed it as their first preference.

I will get a place at one of the schools I put down on the application

This is usually the case but not always. If a parent researches oversubscription criteria and previous demand then this puts them in the position of being able to put schools on their application form that they have a reasonable chance of getting a place at. If this has been done then the chances are that they will get a place at one of the schools they have preferenced. However, if a parent hasn't researched at all and doesn't really understand how the system works they might make unrealistic preferences at schools they have very little chance of securing a place at. If this happens there is a real chance that they wouldn't be offered a place at any of the schools that they put down on the application.

We go to Church so we will get into the Church School

Church Schools do tend to give priority for Church attendance. But it is not guaranteed that going to Church will ensure that you get a place. This is because it would depend on where Church attendance is placed within the oversubscription criteria of the school, whether you can prove your Church attendance so that you can be placed into that criteria and whether your Church attendance has been regular enough over a long enough period of time to qualify for this criteria. If you do qualify for this criteria, qualifying for a place would depend on how many children were ranked above you under the oversubscription criteria.

There will be enough places in the local area for all the local children

This is usually true. Local Education Authorities try very hard to predict future school demand through the study of demographics to look at future population and birth-rates in their area. Unfortunately they do not always get this right, sometimes there can be a sudden change to an area such as a new large housing development that adds a large number of children who require school places to an area. This can dramatically change the need for places in an area. Often Local Education Authorities in this situation will ask local schools to take additional children, sometimes a whole class in a "bulge year". If this does happen it can mean that children who would have got into a school in previous years might not in the bulge year. This is something that can happen, but parents should make their applications as normal as often it is not apparent that it is a bulge year until the applications have been received by the Local Education Authority, or if the Local Education Authority is aware of it usually the parents are not. If at all possible, the Local Education Authority will try to make arrangements to accommodate children if a particular area has a "bulge".

7 SUMMER BORN CHILDREN

<u>Summary</u>

Summer born children are the youngest children in their year group if they go to school at the usual time. Some parents feel that this places the child at a disadvantage and that it is not in the best interests of the child to go to school at that time. Children usually start primary school a year before they reach Compulsory School Age when legally they have to go to school. There is an increasing awareness of this issue and demand from parents for their children to be able to start school at Compulsory School Age in Reception rather than straight into Year 1 as is often the case currently.

Summer borns

There is an increasing awareness of the issue of summer born children. These are defined as children born between 1st April and 31st August. This is currently more of an issue for parents who are applying for their children to start at primary school.

The law states that Admission Authorities must provide for the admission of all children in September following a child's 4th birthday. However, Compulsory School Age (CSA) is from the term immediately following a child's 5th birthday. Legally, children do not have to go to school until they have reached compulsory school age.

The vast majority of parents apply for their child to start school at the usual time, i.e. in the September following the child's 4th birthday. Parents can defer their child's entry until later in that academic year, but not beyond when the child reaches Compulsory School Age, or beyond the start of the final term of the school year for which the offer of a place was made. Children can attend school part-time until reaching compulsory school age.

The issue with summer born children is that some of them may have only turned 4 days before the start of school in September. Many parents of these children feel that they are just not ready to start school at the "normal" time. There has been research to show that summer born children starting at the "normal" time do not do as well as older children starting at that time as they are not sufficiently mature. Some parents do make use of their ability to let their child start later in the school year and / or attend part time until they reach Compulsory School Age.

However some parents do not feel that this is appropriate and wish for their child to start school once they have turned 5 at Compulsory School Age. The problem that has been increasingly in the public domain is that if a parent wishes their child to start at Compulsory School Age, the child is expected to start school with its original cohort (year group)- meaning that they would start school by going straight into Year 1 and missing out on the Reception Year. Many parents do not agree with this because it is widely felt that missing out a whole school year places undue pressure on the child because they have missed everything that the other children learned in their Reception Year. Starting in Year 1 would also mean that a child would be going straight into a class of children who have had a year to make social bonds and friendship groups so it could be harder for them to settle into the class and whole school experience. The other problem with starting in Year 1 is that this would be treated as an In-Year Application rather than being dealt with in the normal admission round. Available school places would be limited as many schools would be full, so parents wishing to do this would have a restricted ability to make preferences as to the school they would wish their child to attend. For all these reasons, an increasing number of parents wish for their child to start school a year later than usual, at Compulsory School Age but to start in Reception rather than in Year 1.

The latest version of the School Admissions Code (2014) made some provisions relating to the admission of children outside their normal year group, particularly summer born children where parents wish the child to start school in Reception a year later at Compulsory School Age rather than at the usual time.

Parents may make an application to the Admission Authority to be able to do this. Admission Authorities have to clearly state in their admission arrangements the process for requesting admission out of the normal age group.

The Admission Authority must make their decision based on the circumstances of each case and the best interests of each child.

In making their decision, the Admission Authority must take account of:

- Parents' views
- Information about the child's academic, social and emotional development
- If appropriate, the child's medical history and views of a medical professional
- Whether the child has previously been educated out with their normal age group
- Whether they may naturally have fallen into a lower age group if they hadn't been born premature

The Admission Authority must also take into account the views of the Head teacher of the school concerned.

If a parent wishes to pursue this option for their child, they should obtain the process that they are required to follow to apply for admission outside the normal age group. It is worth speaking to the Local Education Authority for guidance on this.

It is worth bearing in mind that because the Admission Authority has to take into account the views of the Head teacher of the school, you would need to find out whether the Head teacher would be supportive of entry out with the normal age group. Whether the Head teacher of a school is supportive could be a factor in deciding which schools to preference in your application. As well as the usual research when considering which schools to preference, you would also need to meet with the Head teacher of any school that you liked in order to determine if they would be supportive of your child being admitted to Reception at Compulsory School Age. Remember that although the Local Education Authority is the Admission Authority for Community and Voluntary Controlled Schools (in most cases), it is not for Academies, Foundation Schools and Voluntary Aided Schools. This means depending on the schools you wish to apply for you may be making requests to more than one Admission Authority. It would be common sense to try to secure the support of Head Teachers of more than one school so that you could list a number of preferences in your application to try to maximise the chance of securing a place at a school which was supportive of a Reception start at Compulsory School Age.

The School Admissions Code states that where an admission authority agrees to a parent's request for their child to be admitted out of their normal age group and because of this the child would be admitted to a relevant age group (the age group to which pupils are normally admitted to the school- i.e. Reception)- the application for the place must be processed as part of the main admission round (unless the parental request has been received too late for this to happen). The application must be considered under the same oversubscription criteria as the other applications, and must not be given lower priority because it is for a child being admitted out with their normal age group.

Some Local Authorities currently ask that parents who are applying for a child to be admitted out with their normal age group apply on paper rather than online. This is worth remembering so that you allow extra time to do the application and for it to reach the Local Education

Authority.

Because of the additional time taken to research schools and their Head teachers' attitude towards a child being admitted to Reception at their school out with their normal age group, it would be advisable to start this process sooner rather than later.

One thing to bear in mind if considering this as an option for your child is what might happen when they get to secondary school, particularly if you think you might want them to sit tests for selective schools. It is likely things may change in the next few years if new legislation gives parents the right to choose for their child to start school in Reception at Compulsory School Age, but currently there is no set pathway for these children. Some Local Education Authorities suggest that children could be moved into their usual year group at some point up to starting secondary school or having to sit selective school tests with their usual year group i.e. a year earlier than others in their adopted year group.

It is worth saying that anecdotally, different Local Education Authorities and Admission Authorities around the country have different ways of dealing with the Summer born issue in respect of admission to Reception at Compulsory School Age. At the time of writing, this issue has had much coverage in the press and news. It is widely expected that the School Admissions Code will be revised in the future to give parents the right to choose for their children to enter Reception a year later at Compulsory School Age, rather than is now, some Local Authorities and Admission Authorities permitting this and others not. If this is an issue that you are considering, it is worth researching it further and perhaps joining one of the Summer born Parental Support groups that exist on social media for support and advice from some of the very knowledgeable people who run them.

8 PREPARING TO APPLY

<u>Summary</u>

This chapter gives advice on how to prepare for your school application. Starting early is better than leaving it to the last minute, particularly as this means you would be able to attend any open evenings held by the schools that you are interested in and also give you time to source any evidence you might need such as if you feel your child should be placed into a higher criteria.

It is important to research the schools that you are considering before submitting your application.

Before you start

It is sensible to have a folder to keep all the information you gather together in one place. If you have researched a number of schools and got copies of their oversubscription criteria and their other information it will be easier to find them later on if needed. You can then also put copies of your application together with the proof of receipt by the Local Education Authority into it so that everything is together.

Local Education Authority

The Local Education Authority will have lots of information available about how to apply for a school place in the normal admission round. They will have it on their website but should also have a booklet available for people who cannot access the website. Websites vary between Local Education Authorities; some are excellent with all the information and links to schools laid out very clearly. Others are less clear, but the information will be on there and if anything is unclear you should contact the Admissions Department for the information you require.

The information provided will also give details about how places are allocated by that Local Education Authority in the normal admissions round. It is important to read this so that you understand the system used by your Local Education Authority.

Particular things to find out are:

- The number of preferences you are allowed to list on your application (this differs between LEAs- they must allow three but some allow more)
- The link to register for an online application
- The Admissions Arrangements including Oversubscription Criteria for the Local Education Authority (community schools will come under this)

Many Local Education Authority websites allow users to put in their postcode to view a list of their nearest schools. They often have maps available to view the schools that are available in the Authority area. This is very useful to do as it may show schools that you were not aware of.

Use the information on the website, as well as any schools you were already considering to make a list of the schools which you are interested in.

Find out from the Local Education Authority which your nearest school is. Once you have identified a list of possible schools you would like to apply for you can ask the Local Education Authority to tell you how far away you live from them (using their distance measuring system).

Researching Schools

Once you have your list of possible schools, you will need to find out more information about them.

Things to find out about each school are:

- Distance from you
- Oversubscription criteria (will be on LEA or the school's website)
- Pupil Admission Number
- Details of demand in previous years- was the school oversubscribed? If so you will want to find information about the level of oversubscription the school had in the previous year including the number of applications and the criteria and distance of the last child allocated a place on National Offer Day.

Of course you will also want to research about the ethos and teaching styles / specialities of each school to try to identify the ones that you favour applying for the most.

Look at the school's website. Find it's Admission Policy if it isn't an LEA school and read and understand the oversubscription criteria for the school. If a school is intending on admitting more children than its PAN (this can happen from time to time) it may not appear in the LEA information but should appear on the school's website or be mentioned at the open day.

Once you have all this information you should be able to get a feel for which schools would be realistic choices and which might not be. Of course you may have your heart set on a particular school and be determined to apply for it even if the chances appear slim that you would get a place there. That is fine as long as you understand that the chances are slim and that you consider your other preferences carefully to try and include other schools where you have a better chance of being successful in case you don't get a place at the first preference school. If you get a place at the school you really want despite the chances being slim then that is fantastic, but if not you would want to have got a place at one of your other preferences, rather than putting all your preferences as schools where your chances are slim and not getting any of them.

Visiting the Schools

Once you have done the initial research then hopefully you will have a feel for which schools appeal to you. The next step should be to find out when these schools have their open days / evenings and to attend them. Seeing the schools will give you a better feel for whether you would be happy to list them as preferences, and gives you the opportunity to ask any questions you have about the school. It is also useful to attend open evenings as often they will give more information about any assessment processes (for selective schools or schools using special aptitude as one of their oversubscription criteria) as well as sometimes announcing that they intend to take more children in that year than the published Pupil Admission Number.

Some schools, usually smaller primary schools, don't do open days but instead allow parents to make an appointment to be shown round the school and ask any questions they might have about the school. It is a good idea to do this if an open evening is not being run by the school.

It is up to you whether you take your child along to the open evenings / school appointments. For secondary schools most people do take their children, and they often have their own views about which schools they would like to attend- often influenced by where they think their friends will be going, or if they have a particular favourite subject that a school specialises in. For primary schools, some parents take their children, others don't. Do what you feel is right for you and your family.

Friends and Family

There is no harm in asking friends and family with children at school whether they would recommend the school their child attends if it is one that you might be considering. Parents of children at school can give a different perspective of how schools are run day to day, and how happy their children are at the school and of course their progress. Bear in mind though that different parents at the same school might have different feelings about the school depending on their own circumstances- so take them on board but don't necessarily be put off a school if you happen to come across one person who isn't positive about it.

Social Media

Sometimes people ask for school recommendations on social media. This is understandable as they are usually seeking opinions of parents of children currently at the school. However don't put too much weight on advice from social media. I have seen discussions on social media about schools in my local area where each school mentioned had many parents recommending it (which is a good thing). However for each of those schools I knew at least one set of parents who would disagree with the positive statements made and ended up moving schools. I think this demonstrates how different parents will have different feelings about a school, and the important thing is to try to identify the ones that are most suitable for your child and circumstances for you to put down as realistic preferences.

Oversubscription Criteria

Make sure you have read and understood the oversubscription criteria of the schools that you have identified as possibilities. Try and work out how strong your chances might be of being allocated a place based on the information you obtained regarding demand in previous years and which oversubscription criteria you think your child should be placed in. Remember the information on previous years' demand is only ever an indicator, and not a guarantee as demand does change from year to year. It is however a useful exercise to do to help prevent making completely unrealistic preferences such as listing a school which is always massively oversubscribed and always has a cut off distance of less than 2 miles when you live 7 miles away and would be placed in the last oversubscription criteria. In this example, if you wanted to "have a go" and list it on the off chance then that would be fine as long as you understood your chances would be slim and you put other more realistic preferences down too.

Remember that the cut off distances for primary schools can be very small, sometimes less than a mile if it is a small school in a densely populated area. Cut off distances for large secondary schools however can be much larger if they have a large PAN. You need to research the individual schools that you are interested in to see their cut off distances, remembering of course that demand does change year on year and that they can never be used to say for sure if you would get in- only as an indicator to help you decide which schools may be more realistic to put on your application. If you were applying for a primary school because your child attended their Nursery setting but lived 6 miles outside their catchment area and knew that all the other children attending the Nursery lived well inside the catchment area and were going to apply for that school, your chance of getting a place at that school would be less than if you lived 0.2 miles away from a school whose previous cut off distance was 1.2 miles. These are extreme examples but hopefully illustrate how you can get an idea of how realistic your chances of getting into a school are, remembering of course that demand changes between years so you could never say for sure- it would just be an indication.

Placement in a higher criteria

If you feel that your child should be placed in a higher criteria such as a formerly Looked After Child or exceptional social / medical needs, you will need to find out what information needs to be provided for them to be placed in this criteria. You will have to submit some supporting information, depending on your particular circumstances and the criteria which you feel your child should be placed in. Bear in mind that these applications are often considered by a Panel so it is important to research this well in advance so that you have sufficient time to submit your request and for it to be considered and a decision made.

- -Double check the exact definition given in the Admissions Arrangements.
- -If you feel your child would qualify, contact the Local Education Authority for details of what evidence they require, and the processes involved in submitting it- does it need to be submitted along with your application or beforehand? What process do they have for considering your request for your child to be placed into this criteria- when will it be considered, when

will you be notified of the outcome? All this is essential information which you need to know if you intend to request that your child is placed in a higher criteria.
- -If the schools you are preferencing include schools out with the Local Education Authority that are their own Admission Authority, you should contact them to find out their processes for placing children into higher criteria, the information they require and when they require it by.
- -Clarify the exact processes involved as these can vary between Local Education Authorities and Admission Authorities. If you are preferencing some LEA schools and some others that are their own Admission Authorities- do you have to make the request to both the LEA and the Admission Authority for the other schools, or can this just be done via the LEA? It is important to know exactly who needs what information and when.

Remember the onus is on the parent to provide information and evidence to show that the child should be placed into the higher criteria. If a parent didn't tell the Admission Authority about anything that could qualify the child for the higher criteria, or provide any evidence for this the Admission Authority would not realise there was an issue and would not place the child in the higher criteria which could make the difference between being allocated a place or being unsuccessful.

Supplementary Information Forms

Some schools (particularly Faith schools) require a Supplementary Information Form (SIF) to be submitted along with the standard Local Education Authority application. The information required on the SIFs tends to be required to place children in a higher criteria in the school's Oversubscription Criteria. For example, if a school gives priority to children with regular church attendance, the SIF is likely to ask for details of the church attendance as well as contact details for the church minister. The school would then contact the minister to verify that the church attendance stated on the form is correct before placing a child into the criteria. Not submitting a SIF would mean that a child could be placed in a far lower criteria than had they submitted the SIF which would have proved that they could have gone into a higher criteria such as for regular church attendance. For some schools this could mean the difference between being allocated a place or not. The onus is on the parent to provide the SIF if required.

It is very important to ensure that you know if any of the schools that you are going to preference will also require a SIF. Some Local Education Authority websites are excellent and have downloadable SIFs on the section for each individual school which requires one. They will also allow them to be uploaded as part of the online application process.

Other Local Education Authority websites are less straightforward and may require you to download a form separately, but should state on the school's record that the school requires a SIF. You may need to return the SIF to the school separately.

Always double check on the school's website if they require parents to submit a SIF. It should be stated as part of the Admissions section of their website. The Local Education Authority website should have this information but it is wise to confirm this with the school itself as sometimes the LEA information can be incorrect.

I came across an instance where the information about SIFs being required was incorrect on the LEA's website. In doing the online application for my daughter's primary school, I entered my preferences as normal. In the final summary page of the application, it listed my preferences and for both schools stated SIF required- NO. The first preference school does in fact require a SIF. I only knew this because my older children attend the school and I remembered having to submit a SIF with their applications. Without this prior knowledge of the school (and remembering it because my job gives me an interest in such things) I would not have realised that the SIF was required. In a popular school with lots of applications, depending on the circumstances of the application, this could make the difference between getting a place or not getting a place at the school. Hopefully this example highlights how important it is to double check with the school if a SIF is required, and if so how it should be submitted.

Online application

If you intend to do your application online (this is encouraged by most Local Education Authorities), it is a good idea to familiarise yourself with the system in plenty of time. You will have to register as a user before it will allow you to submit your application. You can do this in advance so it is a good idea to get that part of the process done so that when you are ready to submit your application you can start straightaway. Make sure that you will remember your user name and password when you come to do your application.

Paper application

If you would prefer to do your application on a paper form, you will need to ask the Local Education Authority to send you a copy of the form. Remember to factor in the time that it will take for them to send the form, the time it will take you to do the application, and the time it will take to get to the Local Education Authority once you have posted it when you plan when to ask for the form and do the application. It might be a good idea to request the form when you are contacting the Local Education Authority with your other questions so that you have the form ready for when need it.

Deciding your Preferences

Once you have done all the research into the schools you were considering, you will be ready to decide which ones to preference, and in which order. Things you might like think about when making your decision are:

- -Consider the oversubscription criteria for each school and where you think your child might be placed in these oversubscription criteria. Also consider your distance from each of the schools. This will give you some indication of the likelihood of getting a place at the school. Whilst it cannot be predicted, as demand changes between years (sometimes down as well as up), this is a useful exercise in determining how realistic your chance might be at a particular school. If a school is regularly getting two or three times as many applicants as places, and you live significantly further away from the school than the cut off distance, with your child not being placed in a higher oversubscription criteria, this might indicate that it is a less realistic preference than a school close by which historically has a lower level of demand, particularly if your child might qualify for a higher criteria. Putting a less realistic preference into your application is understandable if you have your heart set on the school but only if you understand that the chance of being allocated a place at the school is less likely, and you compensate for this by putting at least one other preference on the application where you do have a realistic chance of being allocated a place.

- The order in which you preference the schools that you have decided to put in your application. Remember the Local Education Authority will allocate a place at the highest preferenced school at which you qualified for a place. So if you want to put the less realistic but school you have set your heart on in your application, you could consider putting it first. That way if you are lucky and qualify for a place you will be allocated a place at that school. Schools which you might like less than the one you have set your heart on, but have a better chance of getting a place at should go on next. That way if you are unsuccessful in your first preference but successful for the second, you would be allocated a place at the second school. But if you put the school that you are less keen on (but with the better chance of getting a place) first, and qualified for a place at both schools then you would be allocated a place at the school you were less keen on because it was your first preference.

- Your nearest school- many oversubscription criteria give a priority to children for whom the school is their nearest. If it is the school you want most then put it down as your first preference. But if you prefer other schools put them down first. But unless there is a very good reason not to you should put your nearest school down as a preference, even if it is your last preference. This is because if it is your nearest school, you would have a better chance in terms of distance from the school. If the school's oversubscription criteria give priority for being an applicant's nearest school then your chances of gaining a place at the school are increased. Think of it as a backup in case you are unsuccessful in getting places at the other schools you prefer. If you don't get a place at those, at least you have a good chance at getting into the local school. If you don't preference the local school and it fills up with other people who did preference it, if you don't get any of your preferences you will be offered a place at the nearest school which still has space which could be some distance away.

Choice Advisors

Many Local Education Authorities have a team of Choice Advisors who can help parents with their applications- either with researching schools, understanding how the system works or any other issue relating to school applications. If after reading this book you feel you need support with any aspect of your school application, you could contact your Local Education Authority to find out if they have Choice Advisors and if so how to access this service.

9 APPLYING FOR A SCHOOL PLACE

<u>Summary</u>

This chapter gives a checklist of what it is sensible to do in preparing to make your application. It also advises on the application process itself and how to make sure you have sufficient proof of your application in the event of something going wrong and you needing to appeal months later.

Do not leave applying until the last minute! This prevents any panics with online applications on the night of the closing date. It may sound silly but if you have got your application done with a few days to spare, it means any unforeseen problems such as power cuts, internet failure or problems with the online application system that happen while you are applying have got time to be resolved. This is better than any of these things happening during an application made at the last minute where they will cause real stress and panic which as well as being a horrible situation could mean mistakes are made in the application which cause problems later on.

Before you apply

Before you start applying, have your chosen preferences written down in the order that you have decided to put them in your application. Having them written down means you will be able to find the correct school in the application. In a large Local Education Authority with many schools, it is not unusual to have some schools with very similar names (particularly for primary schools) so you want to make sure you pick the correct one from the list. Having the order written down means that you can refer to the list and ensure that you put them in the application in the order that you decided on.

Applying online

If you are applying online, make sure you follow all the instructions on the screen. Leave yourself a bit of time to get the application done rather than rushing. It might be an idea to take some screenshots of your application as you are doing it, but only if you feel you can do this easily without being distracted from the application process. I would definitely take a screenshot of the section with the preferences you have put in and the final screen saying you have completed it. Also print off the confirmation email you will get to say that you have submitted your application. If you don't get this, check your junk email. If it isn't there you will need to double check that the application is fully completed and submitted. Put the screenshots in your application folder in case you need them at a later date. Make sure if your application has needed any additional information such as a SIF or medical evidence, that you have included these with your application. If you have applied with time to spare you could always call the LEA to confirm that they have your application registered and with the right preferences for peace of mind. Make sure you make a note of when you did this and who you spoke to. If you email them to ask for this confirmation, make sure you keep their reply email in your folder as further proof that your application was received.

Paper applications

If you are applying using a paper form, again make sure you have included all the information needed for the schools that you are preferencing such as SIF and medical information. If you can, get a photocopy of everything that you submit. Then post it to your LEA at the address given. Use recorded delivery and keep the tracking information so that you can check that it has been received. You could also include a stamped addressed postcard asking the LEA to post back to you to confirm receipt. If you do this, ensure that you keep the postcard in your application folder to prove that you had submitted the application on time. If the postcard doesn't come back to you, that will tell you that you need to contact the LEA to ensure that they received the application. Although you may have proof of postage, you need to have proof that your application was received by the LEA which is why I would always advise using recorded delivery.

SIFs and Additional Information

If you need to submit a SIF or any additional information, perhaps to support a request for your child to be placed in a higher criteria- make sure that you have proof that it has been sent to the correct place. SIFs often need to be sent to the school, in which case as stated above recorded delivery is a good idea, again keep proof of this in your folder. If it is a local school you could hand deliver and then get them to provide a written receipt for the form which you should keep.

Alternatively, if you are near to the Admissions Offices, you could hand deliver your application. If you do this, make sure that they give you a receipt and keep this in your file.

Again, you could phone the LEA to confirm they have registered it but they can take some time to process and register paper applications so allow a bit of time before you contact them. If you do this, keep a note of who you spoke to and keep it in your file.

It is vitally important that you keep the evidence that you made your application on time and that it was received by the LEA. Put it in your folder for safekeeping. If you end up not being offered a place and you feel that it is because your application was lost or some other error made by the LEA, you will need this evidence for your appeal. It is rare, but occasionally there are mistakes or omissions made by the LEA. In this situation if you have evidence to prove your application was made correctly this will make your case at appeal much stronger as Panels tend to need evidence that applications were received by the LEA if the basis of a case is that it has been lost or some other error made.

If you submit your application early, and then change your mind about your preferences, contact your Local Education Authority about changing them before the closing date. If you do this, make sure that you keep copies of everything as before, particularly if online, screenshots of the new preferences and new confirmation email. I would also check that the LEA has these new preferences on their system.

It is important to note that Local Education Authorities are very aware of the possibility of fraudulent applications being submitted. They use different measures to verify applications and have the power to withdraw places that are offered to applicants who have applied fraudulently, and some will also prosecute applicants who have applied using false information.

Application Checklist

Task	Date done	Notes
Researched schools		
Open evenings / school appointments attended		
Local Education Authority contacted and provided details of nearest school		
Decision made re preferences and their order		
Account registered for online applications		
Checked to see if SIF required		
Checked to find out procedure for submission of any additional information if required		
Application submitted online or on paper		
Proof of receipt by LEA kept and filed		
SIF sent to school if required		
Proof of receipt of SIF kept and filed		

What happens next

Once you have submitted your application, you need to wait until National Offer Day. (1st March for High Schools, 16th April for Primary Schools). These are national dates specified in the School Admissions Code 2014 and the date that Local Education Authorities send out the notification to applicants of the school which they have been allocated. Occasionally LEAs might send out the notification a day or so early if National Offer Day falls on a weekend.

It seems like a long time to wait until National Offer Day, but it will soon pass. Try not to worry about it too much, once you have submitted your application there is nothing you can do other than wait to see what the outcome is. It is a good idea to try not to set your child's heart on a particular school too much by telling them that is where they are going just in case you don't get a place at that school. Hopefully they will and then you can build their excitement about going but if it has been built up before the places have been offered and you don't get a place at your first choice school, it can be distressing for the child.

When you did your application, you may have had the option to sign up for email notification or a letter. Online applicants tend to receive the notification by email. Remember to check your spam folders on your email if you cannot find the email on the day as they can end up in there. If you choose to receive a letter you will receive it in the next few days after National Offer Day as this is the date that the Local Education Authority has to send the letter out so remember it will take time to get to you through the post.

Once you know which school you have been allocated, if you have received your first preference school that is fantastic news. Don't forget to accept the place!

If you didn't get your first preference, you will need to think about what to do next. If you got one of your preferences, consider if you would be happy for your child to attend this school. If you would be, accept the place. You can still appeal for the higher preference school (s) on your application and be on the waiting lists for them, but it is sensible to secure a place at a school that is acceptable to you as back up. If you end up getting a place at a school you prefer, you can just cancel the place at the first school. If you are happy to do this, make sure you accept the place. Further information on what to do if you didn't get a place at the school you wanted is in the next chapter.

10 WHAT TO DO IF YOU DIDN'T GET THE PLACE YOU WANTED

Summary

If you did not get a place at the school you wanted, you need to consider your options. If the place offered is at a school that you would send your child to, it is usually sensible to accept the place. This will not stop you trying to obtain a place at a school you would prefer. Having a place secured at a school that would be acceptable puts you in a much better position than ending up with no place at all at the end of the summer term before your child is due to start.

This chapter explains what you can do to try and improve the school place that you have been offered to one that you are happier with than that initially allocated to you. If you want to do this, it is vitally important that you act quickly. The sooner you act, the better your chance of securing a place at a school you prefer.

If you didn't get a place at your first preference school

If you didn't get a place at your first preference school, you need to think about what to do next. If you were allocated one of your other preferenced schools and you would be happy to send your child there, seriously consider accepting the place. This will ensure that you have a place at a school that is acceptable to you and will not stop you trying to obtain a place at any other schools which you would prefer.

If you didn't get a place at any of your preferences, you need to consider if you would accept the school place offered. Again, if it is one that you would be happy with accept it. You can still try to obtain places at other schools which you would prefer.

Having a place secured at a school which you would send your child to puts you in a much stronger position, and reduces the stress and worry that would occur if you do not have a school place. Think of it as a back-up plan, you can still try to get a place at a school you would prefer, but at least you have one in reserve if needed. If you do secure a place at a school you prefer, you can easily withdraw from the first place.

If you are not willing to accept the school place offered, you need to secure another place. The sooner you start on this, the better your chance of getting a place at a school you would be willing to send your child to. As above, if you get a place at a school quickly that you would accept but have other schools which you would prefer; it is much less stressful if you have a place secured while you try to gain a place at a school you prefer.

Getting a place at another school

The Local Education Authority will have a list of schools that still have places available because they were undersubscribed and weren't filled once all the allocations had been made. Sometimes they will send a copy of the list together with the letter informing you of the school you have been allocated a place at. If they don't, you will need to contact them for the list.

Consider all the schools on the list. If there is one there that you would be happy to send your child to then contact the Local Education Authority to ask for a place at the school. If you can secure a place at a school that you and your child are happy with that early after National Offer Day that is a good thing as you don't need to worry about school places after that. If you want to accept a place at a school but still want to appeal for one or more of your preferred schools you can, but having a school place secured is wise in case you don't win your appeals.

Undersubscribed schools

When considering schools which have been undersubscribed so still have places, you should research them. If you find a school which has just been taken over by an Academy Trust these are always worth looking at carefully. Academy Trusts are growing very quickly at the moment which means they are taking over other schools. Often (but not always) the schools that are taken over may not have been performing as well as other schools in the area and because of this are less popular. If they have been taken over by a large Academy Trust research the Trust and its other schools. If the Trust's other schools are all of good quality with a good ethos and good results then there is a good chance that the Academy Trust will bring the new school up to similar standards as they have set ways of working to achieve high standards that they implement in the schools they take over.

Another type of school that is often undersubscribed is a brand new school. Sometimes schools will open with a reduced PAN and parents are wary of entering it as a preference- either because they have other schools that they know they want to put on their application, or because they don't want to take a risk on a new school. It is worth researching any new schools in this situation, again particularly if they are Academies where you can research the Academy Trust and the standards attained by its other schools. I have watched one new school which only reached half of its PAN at National Offer Day. It filled up over the following few weeks and got to the point where parents were appealing to get into the school. Many parents were those who had been unsuccessful in getting places at the Academy Trust's other more established and hugely oversubscribed schools. If the parents who ended up appealing had acted quickly, they could have got their children a place at the school before it filled up and therefore avoided the stress of appealing which does not guarantee a place being granted at the school.

Waiting Lists

Admission Authorities must keep a waiting list if they are full. This allows them to offer any places that become available to people off the waiting list. Waiting lists are ranked in accordance with the oversubscription criteria used by the school. This means that someone can go up or down on a waiting list depending on who else goes on or off it- if someone who lived closer to the school asked to go onto the waiting list, or who had a sibling at the school, they could go above someone who was already on the waiting list. The School Admissions Code 2014 states that waiting lists have to be ranked according to the oversubscription criteria rather than by the length of time that an applicant has been on the list.

If you want to go onto the waiting lists for the schools you preferenced, or any others, you need to contact your Local Education Authority as quickly as possible. Admission Authorities must keep waiting lists until at least 31st of December of the school year of admission. Many keep them until the end of the school year but it is important to check as they do vary. If you applied to an Academy you may need to contact them directly to go onto the waiting list as Academies are their own Admission Authorities.

Topping Up

Topping up is the process where the Local Education Authority reruns its allocation software to take account of places that have been refused and accepted, and the people who are on waiting lists for the different schools. This tends to be done a couple of weeks after the first National Offer Day (to take account of the places that have been refused and accepted to that point) and thereafter regularly, often weekly.

There will always be people who refuse the place they are allocated. Perhaps they have found a place at a school they prefer (what might be your first preference might be someone else's third preference), or moved out of the area so no longer need a place at the school. Each place that is refused creates a vacant place that can be filled in topping up.

Topping up offers places to people on the waiting lists for the schools. A vacant place would be offered to the applicant at the top of the waiting list as ranked according to the oversubscription criteria.

Chain effect of topping up

If a place becomes available and is offered to another child off the waiting list through topping up, this creates a chain effect. If that child then accepts the place that was offered, this means the place that was originally allocated to them becomes vacant, and is offered to a child on the waiting list for that school. In this way, one child moving out of the area in one area of the city could in effect create a chain effect ending in a place become vacant in a school on the other side of the city once the resulting vacancy has been offered to the child at the top of the waiting list and their original place becoming free and so on. Imagine this happening on a much wider scale with places coming up at many schools and you will see that there is a large degree of "movement" and the potential to be offered a place off the waiting list for schools that were initially oversubscribed. Of course some schools, particularly small local primary schools, may have very little or no movement but other schools may have a large turnover of children being offered places before they start in September. It is impossible to predict how much movement any particular school may have and this can vary between years, but generally speaking there is a large degree of movement in the first few weeks after National Offer Day for applications in the normal admission round which slows down as people accept places that they intend to keep.

Right of Appeal

If you were allocated a school that wasn't your highest preference, or none of your preferences, you have the right to appeal for a place at the schools that you didn't get a place at. Accepting the place that you were offered, or securing a place at another school will not affect your ability to appeal for those schools. It is much better to have a place secured at a school that you would accept as back up in case you don't win your appeals than to wait for the appeals and then find that you have lost them and then have to find a school as many of the schools that would have had places available just after National Offer Day will have filled up by then and there will be far less choice available. If you win your appeal, your "back up" place can be easily cancelled when you accept the place you won at appeal and in the meantime you will have the peace of mind that if you don't win your appeals you already have a school place lined up.

If you wish to Appeal, you will need to inform the Local Education Authority / Admission Authority by their deadline in order to ensure that the appeal is heard within timescales before the end of the school year. Admission Authorities will always try to hear appeals which are submitted after the deadline before the end of the school year (they have timescales they have to meet) but there does come a point where this is no longer possible and the appeals would have to be heard in September once the new school year had started.

I always say that it is worth appealing. Perhaps less so if it turns out to be a Class Size Legislation Appeal (for children starting Primary School- many but not all Reception Appeals will come under this legislation), because these have very restricted grounds on which an appeal can be won, so the chances of success are smaller. But for non Class Size Appeals, or for Secondary Schools, it is definitely worth appealing. Even if you don't actually turn up on the day and allow it to be heard in absence. There is always a slim chance that a Panel might decide that a school has not made a case and if that happens everyone who is appealing in that set of appeals for that school would be granted a place. It doesn't happen very often, but it happens often enough that I would say it is worth a shot. If this doesn't happen, there is still a reasonable chance of success, depending on the strength of your case. The last published statistics at the time of writing (for the 2013/14 academic year) show between a 29%-35% success rate for non Class Size Appeals nationally.

Effect of Admission Appeals on available places

Admission Appeals are run for children who were unsuccessful in the normal admission round. The Appeals have a definite effect on the places that are available to parents who don't wish to appeal.

The positive effect of Admission Appeals is that if a few children are successful and accept the places that they have been granted, this will then generate a number of vacant places that they would have had before at other schools. As already explained this will create a chain effect of places becoming available in other schools as places are accepted, and other places become available as a result of this almost like a ripple effect through the schools in the area and sometimes further.

The negative effect of Admission Appeals is for parents who are on the waiting list for the school that the Admission Appeals are for. Not all parents on the waiting list will choose to appeal. If once the Appeals are heard, a number of children are successful in gaining a place; this will then push the school over its Pupil Admission Number. This means that now instead of a place becoming available to the applicant at the top of the waiting list when a place is given up, the place will not be filled because the school will still be over its PAN and won't have to fill the place. See example below.

Child A- Is at top of waiting list. PAN of 120.

Before the Appeals- if a place becomes available, the school will have 119 children on roll and 1 available place which would be offered to Child A.

After the Appeals- if 6 children win their appeal, the school will have 126 children on roll. The school cannot offer places if it is over its PAN so instead of Child A being offered a place when one child leaves, they will now have to wait until the school drops below its PAN which means 7 children would have to leave before they would be offered a place at the school.

<u>Why you should act quickly</u>

The quicker you act, the better your chance of securing a place at a school you prefer to the one you have been allocated. There are a few reasons for this:

> The sooner you act, the more choice you will have of schools that didn't fill up on initial allocation and that still have spaces left. Many of these will fill up before September so the sooner you act the better chance of getting a place whilst they are still available
>
> -a big one as it will take account of all the places that have been refused for various reasons by the deadline given by the Local Education Authority.

- As time goes on, movement in school places will decrease as the more popular ones gradually fill up reducing what is available to people who haven't yet secured a place they are happy with
- Once a school has had its Admission Appeals, this can push the number of children on roll far above the school's PAN. This then means that no places can be offered until the numbers drop back below the PAN, which is not guaranteed to happen- it is possible that once the appeals have been held no more places will be offered to children off the waiting list because the school won't drop back down below its PAN.

Effect of Topping up and Appealing

It is possible to go through more than one school place between National Offer Day and your child starting school in September. This can be as a result of both topping up and successful appeals. The example below demonstrates how this can happen:

School Place 1- Offered on National Offer Day.

The family were unwilling to send their child to the school offered on National Offer Day. They researched other schools that still had places and secured a place at a new Academy run by a successful Academy Trust that still had places available so gained:

School Place 2- Obtained by the family as a better option than School Place 1

(This school had places available at National Offer Day and the family gained one because they acted quickly, but the school quickly filled up and ended up with appeals by the end of the summer term.

The family still wanted to appeal for the schools which they had preferenced. They appealed for:

Preference 1- but the appeal was unsuccessful so they remained on the waiting list for the school; and

Preference 2- and won their appeal so gained

School Place 3- The family's second preference.

The family were delighted with this and proceeded to prepare their child to go to that school. The week before the new school year started in September, the family received an offer of a place at their first preference school off the waiting list as a number of children had dropped out due to being offered places elsewhere through topping up and places could be offered to children on the waiting list. Therefore the child started school at

<u>School Place 4</u>- which was Preference 1 that they had appealed unsuccessfully for.

This level of movement for one child is unusual, but it demonstrates that movement is possible between National Offer Day and when the children start school in September.

Leaving it too late

Using the example given above, imagine another family who were also allocated School 1, and who also did not want their child to attend that school. They lodged appeals for Preference 1 and Preference 2 and another school, their Preference 3. They had their appeals but were unsuccessful in all of them so were still left with the place at School 1 which they were adamant they didn't want. Once they had lost their appeals, they then researched other schools. They decided they would like to try School 2, but by this time it had filled up with other children. This meant they had to appeal. Unfortunately they lost that appeal too so ended up staying with their originally allocated school, School 1. If they had done as the family in the first example had done, and acted quickly in researching other schools rather than waiting until after they had lodged their appeals, they would have been able to get a place at School 2 with no problem as it had places left for a few weeks at least after National Offer Day.

Hopefully the examples above demonstrate why acting as soon as possible is so important, and can be the difference between getting a place at a school which is acceptable to you, even if it is not one that you preferenced originally, and not being able to get a place at another school.

11 IN-YEAR APPLICATIONS

<u>Summary</u>

When a parent applies for a school place outside the normal admission round, for example if they have moved area and the child needs a new school, this is called an In Year Application. These applications are dealt with differently to those in the normal admission round. This chapter gives information on how to do an In-Year Application (sometimes known as an In-Year Transfer).

In Year Applications

If you want to change your child's school out with the normal admission round, it is a slightly different process. Although Local Education Authorities are not required to co-ordinate In-Year applications, they must provide information on how In-Year applications can be made and will be dealt with.

Local Education Authorities must, on request, provide parents with information about the places still available in all schools within their area, and a suitable form for the parent to complete when applying for a place for their child at any school for which they are not the admission authority.

Parents can apply for a place for their child at any time to any school outside the normal admissions round. If a parent wishes to apply for a school which is its own Admission Authority, they can apply directly to the school for a place (unless the Local Education Authority coordinates all in-year admissions).

Unlike applying for a school place in the normal admission round, you should find out whether your child has a place at the school you have applied for quite quickly as In-Year applications are dealt with individually. Many schools will tell you over the phone if they have a place available in the year group that you need.

Finding a school with a place

Own Admission Authority schools must keep the Local Education Authority updated with any applications they received directly and their outcome. This allows the Local Education Authority to have up to date information on places that are available in the area. If you are looking at changing schools, either due to moving into the area or if your child needs a change of school, it is a good idea to contact the Local Education Authority in the first instance to find out which schools may have places available in the year group for your child.

If you are moving into an area, it is likely that you will want to accept a place at a school quickly so that your child can go to school as soon as possible. Accepting a place doesn't mean you can't be on the waiting list for other schools that you might prefer. You can also appeal for schools that you have asked for a place at that have refused due to being full.

If a school has a place in the right year group for your child, they will usually accept the child. However it is important to note that in some limited circumstances, schools are allowed to refuse a child even if they have a place. Should this happen to you, you would have the right to appeal this decision.

Waiting Lists

If you want your child to attend a school that is currently full, you can go onto the waiting list for the school and you could also submit an appeal for a place at the school once you have been notified that the school cannot take your child.

If a school is full and you have to go onto the waiting list, remember that places that do become available are allocated in line with the oversubscription criteria in the admissions policy for the school. This means that you could go down as well as up on the waiting list if someone else goes onto the waiting list that is ranked above you according to the oversubscription criteria, for example a child with a sibling already attending the school is probably going to be higher on the waiting list than someone who does not come into any particular oversubscription criteria for the school.

It is worth checking with the school how long they operate their waiting list for, they are only required to do this until the 31st December of any school year of admission, but many run them for the whole school year. You are likely to need to reapply if you wish to be placed back on the waiting list in a future school year should a place not have come up in the first school year that you were on the waiting list. Clarify this with the individual school.

Fair Access Protocols

Fair Access Protocols are meant to ensure that unplaced children outside the normal admissions round, especially the vulnerable, are offered a place at a suitable school as quickly as possible. They are also meant to make sure that no one school has to take a disproportionate number of children who have been excluded from other schools or who have challenging behaviour. This means that children can be allocated to schools that are full through the Fair Access Protocol. It is important to emphasise that not all children seeking an In-Year school place will come under Fair Access, only children who come under one of the Fair Access categories.

Put simply, schools are usually organised into groups by location. They will have regular Fair Access meetings where they consider the children in their area who require a place through the Fair Access Protocol. The point of the scheme is to ensure that the children are fairly distributed between schools rather than all being placed in one school that has spaces as this disadvantage that one school by having a disproportionate number of children with challenging behaviour or additional needs. Schools within an area are expected to take "their fair share" of children that are considered through Fair Access, even if they are full in the relevant year groups.

The School Admissions Code 2014 gives set categories of children that Local Authorities have to include within their Fair Access Protocol, and they can then add additional categories to suit their local conditions. The children of compulsory school age who have difficulty in obtaining a school place who must be included within the Fair Access Protocol are listed below:

a). children from the criminal justice system or Pupil Referral Units who need to be reintegrated into mainstream education;

b). children who have been out of mainstream education for two months;

c). children of Gypsies, Roma, Travellers, refugees or asylum seekers;

d). children who are homeless;

e). children with unsupportive family backgrounds for whom a place has not been sought;

f). children who are carers; and

g). children with special educational needs, disabilities or medical conditions (but without a statement or Education, Health and Care Plan).

All Admission Authorities must participate in Fair Access protocols in order to make sure that unplaced children are allocated a school place quickly. Local Education Authorities and Admission Authorities have no duty to comply with parental preference for when allocating places through Fair Access Protocols.

If you think your child should be considered under Fair Access, you should contact your Local Education Authority. It is worth looking up their Fair Access Protocol to see what other categories of children it has stated on its Fair Access Protocol. Not all children will qualify to be considered under Fair Access, but if you feel your child might fit into one of the categories it is worth looking into.

GLOSSARY

Admission Appeal	A hearing that can result in a child being offered a place at the school for which the Appeal is for if the Appeal is upheld.
Admission Authority	The body responsible for setting and applying the school's admission arrangements. For community and voluntary controlled schools, this is the local authority unless it has agreed to delegate responsibility to the governing body. For foundation or voluntary aided schools, this is the governing body of the school. For Academies, this is the Academy Trust.
Admission Arrangements	The overall procedure, practices and oversubscription criteria used in deciding the allocation of school places including any device or means used to determine whether a school place is to be offered.
Admission Number	The number of school places that the Admission Authority must offer in each relevant age group of a school for which it is the Admission Authority. Admission Numbers are part of a school's admission arrangements.
Application	The way a parent or carer expresses a preference for one or more schools for their child, either online or on paper
Catchment area	A geographical area, from which children may be given priority for admission to a specific school. A catchment area is part of a school's admission arrangements.

Closing Date	The date by which applications have to be received by the Local Education Authority in order for them to be considered as on time applications in the Normal Admissions Round
Composite Prospectus	The information that Local Education Authorities must publish online and as hard copies by 12th September in the offer year which contains admissions arrangements and SIFs for state funded schools in the local authority area.
Compulsory School Age	The age at which a child is legally required to attend school. A child reaches compulsory school age on the prescribed day following their fifth birthday (or their fifth birthday if it falls on a prescribed day). The prescribed days are 31st December, 31st March and 31st August.
Co-ordinated admission arrangements	The way in which Local Authorities co-ordinate the distribution of offers of places for schools in their area. All Local Authorities have to co-ordinate the normal admissions round for primary and secondary schools in their area.
Cut off distance	The distance from the school of the address of the last child to be offered a place in the normal admission round.
Education, Health and Care Plan	An Education, Health and Care plan is a plan made by the local authority under Section 37 of the Children and Families Act 2014 specifying the special education provision required for that child.

Fair Access Protocol	A protocol that all Local Authorities must have. It has to be agreed with the majority of schools in the area and is meant to ensure that unplaced children, particularly the most vulnerable, outside the normal admission round are offered a school place as soon as possible.
Feeder School	A school named in the Admission Arrangements as one for whose pupils are afforded a priority in the oversubscription criteria.
First preference first	Oversubscription criteria giving priority to children who have placed the school first; or only considering applications that have named the school as first preference. This is illegal under the School Admissions Code 2014.
Grouped (multiple) Appeals	Appeals usually for the normal admission round (Primary or Secondary schools) which are run so that all appellants are invited to hear the Admission Authority's case together, prior to their own individual appointments to present their case to the Appeal Panel. Multiple Appeals for the same school can run for a number of days.
In Year Appeal	An Appeal for a school place outside the normal admission round - not starting Primary or Secondary School but wishing to change schools at a different time or year group.
Infant Class Size Limit	Legislation limits the size of an infant class (a class in which the majority of children will reach the age of five, size or seven during the school year) to 30 pupils per school teacher.
In-Year Application	Application for a school place out with the Normal Admission Round

Legislation	Law governing School Admissions and School Admission Appeals.
Local Education Authority	The local councils who are responsible for administering the co-ordinated admission arrangements within their areas for school applications in the normal admission round.
Local Government Ombudsman	An independent, impartial and free service that investigates complaints about maladministration of certain public bodies.
Looked after child (and previously looked after children)	A 'looked after child' is a child who is (a) in the care of a local authority, or (b) being provided with accommodation by a local authority in the exercise of their social services functions (see the definition in Section 22(1) of the Children Act 1989) at the time of making an application to a school. Previously looked after children are children who were looked after, but ceased to be so because they were adopted (or became subject to a child arrangements order or special guardianship order.
National Offer Day	The day each year on which Local Authorities are required to send the offer of a school place to all parents of school pupils in their area. For secondary pupils, offers are sent out on 1st March. For primary pupils offers are sent out on 16th April.
Normal Admissions Round	The period during which parents are invited to express at least three preferences for a place at any state-funded school, in order of preference for children starting Reception or Secondary School. The deadlines for applications are 31st October for secondary school places and 15th January for Primary school places.

Oversubscription Oversubscribed	Where the number of applicants for places is higher than the school's published admission number.
Oversubscription Criteria	The published criteria that the Admission Authority applies when a school has more applications than places available in order to determine which children are offered places.
Published Admission Number	The number of school places that the Admission Authority must offer in each relevant age group of a school for which it is the Admission Authority. Admission Numbers are part of a school's admission arrangements.
Ranking	The process where all the applications for a school are ordered by applying the oversubscription criteria of the school to determine which children would qualify for a place at the school.
School Admissions Code 2014	The current legislation governing School Admissions. It came into force on 19th December 2014.
Schools Adjudicator	A statutory office holder who is independent of but appointed by the Secretary of State. Decides on objections to published admission arrangements.
Selective School	Schools which are allowed to select their entire intake on the basis of high academic ability and who do not have to fill all of their places if they have insufficient applicants of the required standard.

Statement of Special Educational Needs	A Statement of Special Educational Need is a statement made by the local authority under Section 324 of the Education Act 1996 specifying the special educational provision required for that child.
Summer born	A child who was born between 1st April and 31st August.
Topping up	This is a term used for the offers of places made to children on the waiting list for a school after the initial allocation of school places. If a place becomes available at a school then it is offered to the highest placed child on the waiting list by "topping up".
Undersubscription Undersubscribed	Where the number of applicants for places at a school is less than the total number of places available for that year group
Waiting List	The list of children held and maintained by the Admission Authority when the school has allocated all of the places, on which the children are ranked in priority order against the school's published oversubscription criteria.

ABOUT THE AUTHOR

The author has extensive experience working in School Appeals, from clerking individual School Appeals to being responsible for the overall running and co-ordination of the School Appeals Service of a large Local Authority. The author now runs their own Admission Appeal service and is also an experienced Independent Admission Appeals Panel Member.

SCHOOL APPEALS EXPLAINED

J. TOMLINSON

Copyright © 2015 J. TOMLINSON

All rights reserved.

ISBN-13: 978-1512052473

ISBN-10: 151 2052477

CONTENTS

Introduction

1	Why didn't my child get a place at the school I asked for?	3
2	School Admission Appeals	13
3	Appeal Types and Methods	23
4	Decision Making Process of the Appeal Panel	29
5	So you want to Appeal- what happens now?	39
6	Preparing for your Appeal- Submitting Evidence	43
7	Preparing for your Appeal- The Admission Authority's Case	51
8	Preparing for your Appeal- Your Case	61
9	The Appeal Hearing	67
10	After the Appeal	71
	Glossary	75
	Appendix A	83
	Appendix B	85
	Appendix C	87

INTRODUCTION

Considering whether to appeal after your child has been refused a place at a school can be a daunting prospect for parents if they have not had experience of Admission Appeals before. This book aims to demystify the process so that parents and carers can understand what happens at an Admission Appeal, from what happens on the day itself, to the legislation under which an Appeal is decided, and guidance on how to prepare their case for the Appeal. This book also explains the different sorts of Admission Appeals, as well as the different ways that Admission Appeals can be conducted. This will give parents and carers the confidence to make an informed decision on whether they wish to appeal, and if they do decide to go ahead they will know what to expect on the day as well as the knowledge of how to prepare for their appeal to maximise the chances of winning it. Each chapter has a helpful summary of the information it covers.

There is also an explanation of how places at schools are allocated, and possible reasons why a child may not have got a place at the school requested. This will give parents an understanding of how the allocation process works which will help them in finding the best available schooling option for their child, and be useful knowledge should they decide to Appeal.

Demand for school places is set to increase. Increasing pressure on school places will mean fewer children will be allocated the school that their parents would choose first. This means that the prospect of an Admission Appeal will become more common.

1 WHY DIDN'T MY CHILD GET A PLACE AT THE SCHOOL I ASKED FOR

Summary

All Schools have a certain number of children which they are allowed to accept for each year group. If less children than this apply in the normal admission round then all the children must be offered a place. But if more children apply than are places, not all of the children can be offered a place. The Admission Policy sets out different categories in which children are placed and this is how it is decided which children are offered a place at the school.

If a child is refused a place that they applied for, they have the right to Appeal. This applies to applications for children starting Primary and Secondary School and also for those seeking to change school at other times.

Accepting the place you were offered when you were applying for your child to start Primary or Secondary School, if it is one that you would send your child to means that you have a place secured in case you do not win your Appeal. Accepting the place at this stage does not change your chances of winning your Appeal.

How School Places are allocated

All places at schools have to be allocated using the Admission Authority's Admission Policy. Different Admission Authorities can have different Admission Policies, but there are strict rules to ensure that consultation is done in advance of changes being implemented, and they have to be approved by the Schools Adjudicator before they come into force. An Admission Authority can be the Local Education Authority for Council run schools, or other schools, such as Academies can themselves be the Admission Authority and have their own Admissions Policy. The Law governing this is the School Admissions Code 2012 for admissions up to 2015/16. For admissions in 2016/17 and onwards, the School Admissions Code 2014 applies. The School Admission Code states that all children whose statement of special educational needs (SEN) or Education, Health and Care (EHC) plan names the school must be admitted.

All Admission Authorities must have a Published Admission Number which is the number of children they can admit in each year group.

All Admissions Policies have set categories in which children are placed when they apply for a place. These are called oversubscription criteria and determine how children are ranked and which ones are allocated places at the school if the school is oversubscribed, i.e. there are more children asking for a place than there are places. If the school is not oversubscribed, so there are more places available than requested, all children who applied in the normal admission round must be offered a place at the school. If there are more applications than places, then not all of the children will be offered a place. The Admissions Policy is used by the Admission Authority to determine which children are offered places by being used to rank applications in order against its published oversubscription criteria. The law requires that the highest priority be given to looked after children, and previously looked after children. After children in this category, the oversubscription criteria must then be applied to all other applicants in the order set out in the Admissions Policy.

Different types of school can have different Admissions Policies. One example is faith schools which often give regular church goers a higher priority under their Admissions Policy than non-church goers, or baptised Catholics being given a higher priority than non-baptised Catholics for Catholic faith schools. Some schools ask for additional information from the parent to prove that a child should be placed in a higher criteria, for example a faith school wishing to get further information about a child's church attendance or proof of a child's baptism. If the additional information is not provided, it can mean that the child is placed in a lower criteria than the parents might have expected as the school didn't receive sufficient proof to place them in the higher criteria. This can then mean that the child doesn't get a place at the school due to being placed into a lower criteria than they would have been should the required information been provided at the time of application.

Some often used criteria are listed below:

- Siblings at the School: The Admission Policy must clearly state what is considered as a "sibling" for example older brothers or sisters, half brothers or sisters, step siblings, foster siblings living at the same address, but not other family members such as cousins who live at the same address.
- Distance from the School: The Admission Policy must specify how the distance will be measured- some Authorities use a straight line distance, others use distance by road. The points that the measurement will be taken from must also be specified, for example from the home address to the centre of the main school building. Many Admission Authorities have specialist mapping software which they use to determine the distances.

- Catchment Areas: This criteria is often, but not always used. They must be designed so that they are reasonable and are clearly defined. Parents who live outside the catchment area of a particular school are still able to express a preference for the school.
- Feeder Schools: Some Admission Authorities give priority to children attending a particular school which is named as a Feeder School. This must be clearly stated in the Admission Policy and be reasonable.
- Social and Medical Need: Admissions Authorities using this criteria must set out clearly how they will define this need, and specify what supporting evidence would need to be submitted as proof.
- Nearest school: Some Admission Authorities give a higher priority to children for whom the school is their nearest school. If this is the case it is important to see how this is worded as the exact way in which it is applied can vary between Admission Authorities.

Parents / carers have the right to appeal against the decision of the Admission Authority to refuse admission to their child to the school that they applied for. The Admission Authority must set out the reasons for their decision to refuse admission, and inform of the right of appeal and the Appeal process.

Choice vs Preference

When parents talk about the application they have submitted for their child's school place, they often talk about "choices" they have put down. When Admission Authorities talk about the applications they have received for places at a school, they talk about "preferences".

Choice and Preference are not the same, and it is important to understand the difference between the two in order to have a better understanding of how school Admissions work.

Legally, parents have the right to "express a preference" for a school which is what they do when they name the schools on their application for a school place. For applications to start Reception or Secondary school, the Local Authority co-ordinates the allocation of places and is required to offer parents a place at the highest preference school on their application at which a place is available. If schools are popular and there are more applications than places, not all children will get a place at the school. This means that although sometimes parents believe that if they have put a particular school on an application, they will get a place there because they "chose" it, this is unfortunately not always the case. Instead, Local Authorities have to have regard to parental preferences when allocating places to ensure that the parents are offered a place at their highest preference school, but this does not always guarantee that a place will be offered at a school preferenced by a parent.

The way in which places are allocated to applicants is explained later in this chapter.

Starting Primary or High School

When applying for a place for a child to start Primary or Secondary School, there is a defined application process with key dates. Applying on time or applying late can make the difference between a child getting a place at a school or not.

When the Admission Authority has all the applications in after the closing date, the children are placed in the correct over subscription category as stated in the Admission Policy. The children are then ranked using the oversubscription criteria. If there are more places than children applying for a place, all children would be offered a place. However if a school is oversubscribed (more children applying for places than the Published Admission Number), the Admissions Policy will determine which children are offered places. Starting at the top criteria (looked after children and previously looked after children), all children are offered a place until the places are all used. If there are spaces for some but not all children within a particular category, the children in this category may be ranked such as by distance. For example if some but not all children in the Siblings category would be offered places, it may then be decided on the distance from the school of the child's home, with the places going to the nearest children within that category. Or the allocation could go further down the categories, to children without siblings, who could be ranked on distance. Again, the nearest children within that category would be offered the remaining places if this is how the oversubscription criteria work for the Admission Policy.

If a late application is made after the places have been allocated, that child wouldn't receive a place if all places available had been already allocated as there would be no places left. This can lead to a situation where a child who would have been in a high category such as with a sibling at the school wouldn't be offered a place, despite other children of lower categories being offered places, because their applications were submitted on time. This is why it is so important to make sure applications are done on time. However, this child would be likely to be high up in the waiting list in case a place became available after the initial offers are made (for example if a child moves out of the area, or if they are allocated a place at a higher preference school either through successful appeal or off the waiting list).

If you did not receive a place at the Reception or Secondary School you put first in your preferences, it is very important to decide how you wish to proceed. If you want to Appeal, this gives you a chance of being granted a place at the School via the Appeal process. However, this is not guaranteed, so you need to think about a back-up plan should you not win your Appeal. If you were offered the school you put as a second preference, and this is a school that you would send your child to, you should seriously consider accepting the place. This is very important as it means that you have a place at a school which is acceptable to you even if it was not your first preference. You can ask to be put onto the waiting list for any schools, and if you do decide to Appeal you would automatically be placed onto the waiting list for that school. Children are often offered places through "Topping Up" where if a place becomes available it is offered to the highest child on the waiting list. If this happens to a child who is scheduled for an Appeal for the school that they are being offered, the Appeal would be cancelled.

You do not want to end up in the situation where you didn't accept any of the places offered and then find that you have not been granted the place you appealed for. The reason for this is that there is a lot of movement in terms of school places soon after they are allocated, but by the time the Appeal results are known, most schools will have filled up even if they were not full immediately after the places were offered on the National Offer Day. Waiting until after the outcome of the Appeal is known could mean you no longer have the opportunity to get a place at an alternative school which you might have accepted and there are only very limited options left open to you. If you accept the place that you were offered, this will be cancelled should you gain a place at your preferred school at Appeal.

Accepting the school place makes no difference to your chance of succeeding at your Appeal, and Appeal Panel members understand that accepting a place in this way is a sensible way to make sure your child has a place at an acceptable school while still pursuing your right to Appeal for your preferred school. Local Authorities would advise parents in this situation to accept the place. It is very important if you are going to accept the school place to do this before the deadline stated on your offer letter otherwise the place could be allocated to another child and you would lose the place.

If you would not consider sending your child to the school which you were offered, you need to look at expanding your preferences to include schools you would accept. That way you have the fall back position of a place at a school which you would send your child to with the possibility of still gaining a place at the preferred school either via the waiting list or following the Appeals hearing. If you are in this position, it is advisable to contact your Local Education Authority for advice and details of schools that do have places available. It is important to do this as soon as possible after receiving your initial offer letter to give you the best chance of finding a school that is acceptable to you that does have places available as they do tend to fill up as many parents are doing the same thing. You can also ask to be put onto the waiting list for other schools that don't have places available. There is often movement in school places in the summer term after the offers have been made as even one child turning down a school place, perhaps because they are moving out of the area, can have a ripple effect as that school place being offered to another child off their waiting list frees up a place at another school and so on.

In Year Applications

In Year Applications are where a place is requested at a school out with the normal admission round. This means any requests for a school place other than the usual applications to start Primary or High School. Applying In Year is often if a family has just moved to a new area and need a school there, but can be for other reasons such as if a child is being bullied at a school, or if the parents feel that the school requested would meet their child's needs better.

If a place is requested, in most cases the school should offer a place if there is one available (although in some limited circumstances they can refuse). If the year group requested is full however, a place cannot be offered as the school is not allowed to accept more children than the Pupil Admission Number. If a place becomes available, the place must be offered in line with the Admissions Policy. This means the Admissions Policy must be applied to all the children on the waiting list for a place in that year group to rank the children by the oversubscription criteria, and the place would be offered to the child at the top of the list. It is important to note that a child's place on the waiting list for a school can go down as well as up. If a child who lived closer to the school went on the waiting list, and if distance was one of the oversubscription criteria, that child would be placed higher up the waiting list than a child living further away even if they had been on the waiting list for longer.

2 SCHOOL ADMISSION APPEALS

Summary

School Admission Appeals are hearings where parents can appeal the decision not to be given a place at the school they expressed a preference for. Appeal Panels have the power to grant a place at the school. School Admission Appeals are governed by the School Admission Appeals Code 2012.

There are a number of different people involved in any Appeal hearing.

There is a set decision making process with a number of elements which have to be considered by the Appeal Panel as they make the decision whether to grant or refuse the Appeal.

There are specific timescales which apply to School Admission Appeals.

What is an Admission Appeal?

An Admission Appeal is a hearing where parents / carers of a child who was refused a place at a school that they applied for can ask that the child be granted a place at the school. The Appeal Panel can overturn the decision of the Admission Authority not to offer a child a place, and therefore grant a place at the school for the child. The Appeal Panel is made up of Panel Members who are independent of the Admission Authority and the School. If a parent has applied for a place at a school for their child, they have the right to Appeal if they were refused a place. It is the Appeal Panel that will decide if the Appeal will be upheld (granted) or refused. Their decision is binding upon the school, therefore if the appeal is upheld, the school must admit the child.

The School Admission Appeals Code 2012 states that "Appeal panels must operate according the principles of natural justice. Those most relevant to appeals are:

a). members of the panel must not have a vested interest in the outcome, or any involvement in an earlier stage, of the proceedings;

b). each side must be given the opportunity to state their case without unreasonable interruption; and

c). written material and evidence must have been seen by all parties"

In 2013/14, a total of 50,550 Admission Appeals were lodged by 1st September of that year for a place relating into entry at the start of the academic year. 36,965 of these Appeals went on to be heard. 26.7% of Secondary School Appeals were upheld. For Primary Schools, the overall number of upheld Appeals was 19.6% (Infant classes of which some but not all came under Class Size Legislation had 13.7% of Appeals upheld; Appeals for all other Primary School years had 34% upheld). These figures do not include Appeals lodged in relation to applications for children wishing to move schools within the year are not included in these figures.

Who provides the School Appeal?

For many schools, the Appeal is provided by the Local Education Authority. This means the Appeal is administered by the local Council. Sometimes Academies have their Appeals administered by the Council. For Academies and other schools which are their own admitting authority, they can provide their own Appeals Service which must comply with the same legislative requirements as set out in the School Admission Appeals Code.

The Right to Appeal

If a parent has applied for a place for their child at a school which has been refused, the refusal letter must state the parents' right to Appeal and give details on how to do this including contact details and the deadline for lodging an appeal. Parents must be informed that if they wish to appeal, they must set out their grounds for appeal in writing, and Admission Authorities cannot limit the reasons for which an appeal can be made. The refusal letter must state why the application for a place was refused.

Timescales

Admission Authorities must set a timetable for their Admission Appeals, which has to be published on their website by 28th February every year. This timetable must ensure that:

- The deadline given for lodging an appeal gives the appellants at least 20 school days from the date they were notified that their application for a place was unsuccessful to prepare and submit their written appeal.
- Appellants must receive 10 school days notice of their appeal hearing.

- Reasonable deadlines are given to appellants to submit additional evidence and for admission authorities to submit their evidence to allow the Clerk to provide the required information to the appellants and Appeal Panel so that all parties have a reasonable time to read it before the Appeal hearing.

Admission Appeals must be heard within certain timescales:

- For applications made in the normal admissions round (for children starting primary or high school), appeals must be heard within 40 school days of the deadline given by the Admission Authority for lodging appeals.
- For late applications the appeal should be held within 40 school days of the original deadline if possible, or within 30 school days of the appeal being lodged.
- For in-year appeals, the appeal must be heard within 30 school days of the appeal being lodged with the Admission Authority.

Any appeals which are lodged after the deadline given must still be heard in accordance with the timescales set out by the Admission Authority's published timetable.

Once the Appeal is heard, the law states that letters stating the decision of the Appeal Panel should be sent to appellants within five school days if possible.

Venue

The law states that the venue used for Admission Appeals must be appropriate, accessible to appellants and has suitable waiting areas to allow the appellants and presenting officers to wait separately from the panel before and between appeals. Appeals are often heard in Council buildings such as Town Halls. Other venues often used for Appeals are conference facilities in hotels, village halls (as long as requirements for separate waiting areas are met), or even sometimes at the schools themselves if they have appropriate meeting rooms or offices.

Appeal hearings must be heard in private (except for the first stage of multiple grouped appeals). One party (appellant or presenting officer) must never be left alone with the Appeal Panel without the other. If only one party has attended, the clerk must remain with the Appeal Panel at all times throughout the Appeal Process.

Who is involved in an Admission Appeal

A number of different people are involved in an Admission Appeal:

- Clerk
- Presenting Officer
- Appeal Panel Members
-

In addition, sometimes the following people can be present, but not always
- School Representative
- Observer
- Legal representative

The appellant might also have the following people if they wish

- Interpreter
- Support person

<u>The Clerk</u>

The Clerk must be independent of the Admission Authority and school. The Clerk must have knowledge of the School Admissions Appeals Code, the School Admissions Code and other law relating to admissions and other relevant law, and be able to offer advice to enable the Appeals Panel to undertake its judicial function. They provide an independent and impartial service. The Clerk is responsible for the smooth running of the appeals process, from scheduling the appeals, appointing the Panel Members who will sit on the Appeal Panel in accordance with the requirements of the School Admissions Appeals Code, sending out the invitation letters and accompanying information to the appellants, collating and sending out evidence to all parties, advising appellants on the appeals process as required, clerking the Appeal hearings, keeping a comprehensive record of the proceedings and writing and sending out the decision letters and accompanying information after the Appeals. They ensure that the Panel Members make their decisions in accordance with the School Admission Appeals Code and provide procedural advice as required. The Clerk also ensures that the Panel Members are appropriately trained before appointing them to form part of an Appeals Panel. The Clerk is the person that the appellants are likely to deal with the most throughout the Appeals process.

Presenting Officer

The Presenting Officer is provided by the Admission Authority to present the reasons as to why the child was refused the place at the school. They answer questions from the appellants and Panel regarding the information they have presented, and also about the Statement of Case that is sent out to parties prior to the Appeal hearing which gives detailed reasons about why an additional child cannot be admitted to the school.

Appeal Panel Members

The Appeal Panel Members are appointed by the Admission Authority, or more usually, the Clerk to the Admission Appeals. They are independent of the Admissions Authority and the school for whom the Appeals are for. The Appeals Panel is usually three members.

The Appeal Panel is comprised of a Chair and two (if the Panel is of three Members) other Panel Members. Panel Members fall into two categories:

- Lay- someone without personal experience in the management of any school or the provision of education in any school (except as a school governor or in another voluntary capacity)
- Education- someone who has experience in education, who is acquainted with educational conditions in the local authority area, or who is the parent of a registered pupil at school.

The Appeal Panel must have one person from each category, plus one more member who can come from either category.

Admission Authorities have to ensure that Panel Members are independent of the Admission Authority and School and retain their independence for the duration of the time that they are

serving Panel Members for them.

Some people cannot be members of an Appeal Panel. The Clerk is responsible for ensuring that people who can't be members of an Appeal Panel are not appointed as such. People who cannot serve on an Appeal Panel are disqualified and the reasons for disqualification are:

- A member (Councillor) of the local authority which is the admission authority or in whose area that the school is located;
- A member or former member of the governing body of the school in question;
- Employed by the local authority or governing body of the school in question other than as a teacher or teaching assistant (but those employed as teachers or teaching assistants would not be able to form part of an Appeal Panel for the school that they work);
- Any person who has, or at any time has had, any connection with the authority, school, or any persons as detailed above which could reasonably be taken to raise

- doubts about that person's ability to act impartially during the Appeals process;
- Any person who has not attended training required by the admission authority arranging the Appeal Panel.

One Panel Member will be the Chair of the Appeal hearings

Chair

The Chair is responsible for ensuring the smooth running of the Appeal hearings. They will introduce all parties present at the start of the hearings, explain the roles of the clerk and panel, explain how the hearing will be conducted and ensure that all parties have the opportunity to present their case to the Panel and ask questions. A good Chair will make sure that appellants

understand the process, and feel comfortable to ask should there be something they are not sure about during the hearing. They should also ensure that appellants leave the Appeal hearing feeling that they got the chance to say everything that they wished to, and understood the process.

School Representative

If the Presenting Officer is not from the school that the Appeal is about, sometimes the School will send a representative to the Appeal. Their role is to answer detailed questions from the appellants or Panel about the school if required. If there is a separate Presenting Officer, the School Representative's role is purely to answer questions.

Observer

Sometimes there will be an Observer at an Appeal hearing. This is usually someone learning to do one of the roles involved in an Appeal hearing (e.g. Clerk / Presenting Officer / Panel Member). They play no part in the Appeal hearing or decision making process. Appellants are usually asked prior to the appeal if they mind an observer being present.

Legal Representative

Very occasionally, the Appeal Panel may request a Legal Representative to attend the Appeal to provide them with advice.

Interpreter

If the appellant does not speak English well, many Admission Appeals have the facility to provide an interpreter for the hearing. If this facility is available, there is usually a question on the Appeals Form asking if an interpreter is required, and in which language. Sometimes an appellant will bring along a friend or family member to help them with English.

Support for the Appellant

The appellant can bring along another person with them to support them with the Appeal Hearing. This could be a friend or family member. It could also be a professional such as a Social Worker or Solicitor. The appellant could ask their support person to present their case for them, or just answer questions, or just be there for moral support. Appellants are asked to inform the Admission Authority / Clerk should they intend to be represented at the Appeal Hearing.

What Happens in a School Appeal

The Clerk must notify the appellants of the order of proceedings in advance of the appeal. This usually means that an information leaflet giving details of this, and other information is sent out with the letter notifying appellants of the date and time of their appeal.

For most appeals, the Appeal hearing is done in this order:

- The Presenting Officer presents the case for the admission authority
- The appellants and Appeal Panel question the Presenting Officer about what they have said, and also about information sent out in advance of the appeal
- The appellant presents their case as to why they feel their child should be granted a place at the school that they are appealing for
- The Appeal Panel and presenting officer can ask the appellants about what they have said
- The Presenting Officer sums up their case for the admission authority
- The appellants sum up their case

The Chair would ensure that prior to this, all parties are introduced to each other and that all parties are told that they can ask if they are unsure of anything during the Appeal hearing.

This is the order in which individual Appeals are held. It is varied slightly for grouped multiple Appeals.

Admission Appeals can vary in their duration, but typically between 20 and 40 minutes is allocated for each on depending on if it is a grouped or individual Appeal. You should feel that you got the chance to say everything that you wished to and shouldn't feel rushed.

3 APPEAL TYPES AND METHODS

Summary

There are different types of Admission Appeals:

- Appeals in the normal Admission Round
- In Year Appeals
- Infant Class Size Appeals
- Fair Access Appeals

Different Legislation applies to Infant Class Size Appeals.

Appeals can be done in either of the two methods:

- Individual Appeals
- Grouped Appeals

Types of Admission Appeal

Appeals in the normal Admission Round-

These are for places for children starting Primary or Secondary School so Reception or Year 7. Often run in the Grouped Method due to the volumes concerned.

In Year Appeals

Appeals for places in other year groups, or outwith the normal admission round, for example if a family has moved into an area and the school they wish their children to attend is full in the year group that their child is in. Usually run individually but sometimes can be done using the Grouped Method if there are a number of In Year Appeals scheduled for the same school.

Infant Class Size Appeals

Infant Class Size Legislation applies to Infant classes where the majority of children will reach the age of 5, 6 or 7 during the school year. In practice, this usually means Key Stage 1; Reception, Year 1 and Year 2. This means that except for very limited circumstances, the class sizes are limited to 30 pupils per school teacher. A list of "excepted children"- children who when they are added to a class make it exceed 30 children, can be found in Appendix A.

Sometimes, an Appeal can come under "future Class Size Legislation". This would occur when although the year group that the appeal is for doesn't come under class size, it would fall under this as the cohort moves into a future year group. This tends to happen with schools that have mixed classes with more than one year group of children in them. The Appeal Panel would have to establish if this was the case in deciding the Appeal.

An Infant Class Size appeal is where "an admission authority refuses to admit a child on the grounds that the admission of an additional child would breach the infant class size limit and there are no measures it could take to avoid this without prejudicing the provision of efficient education or efficient use of resources".

The key difference between Infant Class Size Appeals and other Appeals is that the Appeal Panel only has very limited grounds on which they can grant the appeal.

Appeals can be done either individually, or as Multiple Grouped Appeals (usually for large numbers of Appeals for entry into Reception)

Fair Access Appeals

The School Admissions Code requires Local Authorities to have a Fair Access Protocol. These are intended to ensure that, outside the normal admissions round, a place at a suitable school is provided quickly for children without a school place, particularly the most vulnerable children. It also requires Local Authorities to ensure that no one school is required to take a disproportionate number of children with challenging behaviour. In circumstances set out in its Local Authority's Fair Access Protocol, an Admission Authority may refuse to admit a child outside the normal admissions round, even if there are places available in the relevant year group on the grounds that admission of the child would prejudice the provision of efficient education or efficient use of resources at the school. A list of the mandatory Fair Access Protocol categories can be found in Appendix C. Local Authorities can add more categories to their Fair Access Protocol.

If a parent / carer is dissatisfied with the place allocated to them under the Fair Access Protocol, they have the right of Appeal against refusal of a place at the school(s) for which they applied. If the place at the school they applied for was refused despite there being places available in that year group, the Appeal Panel must take into account the requirements set out in the Local Authority's Fair Access Protocol, as well as whether the Presenting

Officer has clearly demonstrated that the admission of the child would be prejudicial to the school or other children.

Different Appeal Methods

Individual Appeals

For individual appeals, all appellants have an individual appointment time. They might be part of a day of appeals for the same school / year group, or depending on the size of the Admission Authority, be part of a day of appeals for various schools and year groups. The Clerk would meet the appellants in the waiting area and introduce them to the Presenting Officer (and School Representative if present) before taking all parties into the room where the Appeal is to be held. The Appeal Panel would already be in the room. The Appeal would then be conducted in the order specified above. If there is more than one Appeal in a session for the same school and year group, the Panel cannot decide whether any should be upheld or refused until all of the Appeals have been heard.

Multiple Grouped Appeals

Appeals tend to be done using the Grouped Method when there are a large number of Appeals for one year group at a particular school. This most often occurs for Appeals in the normal Admission Round, i.e. people appealing for places in Reception or Year 7 as they were not offered a place at the school for which they expressed a preference for when applying for their child starting at Primary School or Secondary School.

The Grouped Method is different to the Individual Appeals Method because the Presenting Officer presents the School's case to all the appellants together. All appellants are invited to the Schools Case (Stage 1 hearing) and are also given another appointment time for them to present their case to the Appeal

Panel in private. Sometimes the Stage 1 part of the Appeal is held twice to give maximum opportunity for appellants to be able to attend.

The Grouped Method is designed to hear the Appeals in a more efficient way, allowing more Appeals to be heard in one day than if they were done individually. This is because the School's Case is only made once or twice rather than in every Appeal hearing. This allows for a shorter time to be scheduled for each individual Appeal hearing as they will not need to include presenting the School's Case in the hearing. If a school has 80 appeals for its Year 7 intake, this is an important consideration for the efficient running of the Appeals. Another benefit of the Grouped Method is that it allows all the appellants to hear each other's questions and arguments with respect to the School's Case which many appellants feel gives them increased confidence to ask questions and challenge the School's Case.

It is rare, but possible, for an Appeal Panel to dismiss the School's Case at Stage 1 and uphold all of the Appeals without proceeding to Stage 2. If this happened, the Chair would inform all appellants at the Stage 1 hearing. This is unusual, but does happen from time to time. This would only happen if the Appeal Panel determined that the School did not have a Case, and that it would not cause prejudice to the school if all of the children for whom the appeals were for were admitted to the school. If the Appeal Panel found that there were more appellants than they felt could be admitted to the school without causing prejudice, they would have to proceed to Stage 2. This would allow the Appeal Panel to determine which appellants had the strongest cases before granting the number that they felt could be admitted without causing prejudice to the school.

As for Individual Appeals for the same school and year group, the Appeal Panel cannot make any decisions on any of the Appeals until they have all been heard. This means that if an appellant has their Appeal on the first day of a Multiple Grouped Appeal which runs for several days, a decision won't be made on their case for a few days afterwards, so it will take longer for them to find out the outcome of their Appeal.

---

4 DECISION MAKING PROCESS OF THE APPEAL PANEL

Summary

The Appeal Panel has to follow a specific order in deciding the outcome of an Admission Appeal. The decision making process for an individual Appeal is illustrated in the flowchart. Appeal decisions are made in a two stage process.

Infant Class Size Appeals are dealt with differently, and the Appeal Panel is restricted by legislation which only gives three reasons that allow an Appeal Panel to grant an Appeal.

Admission Appeal Decision Making Process
Individual Appeals

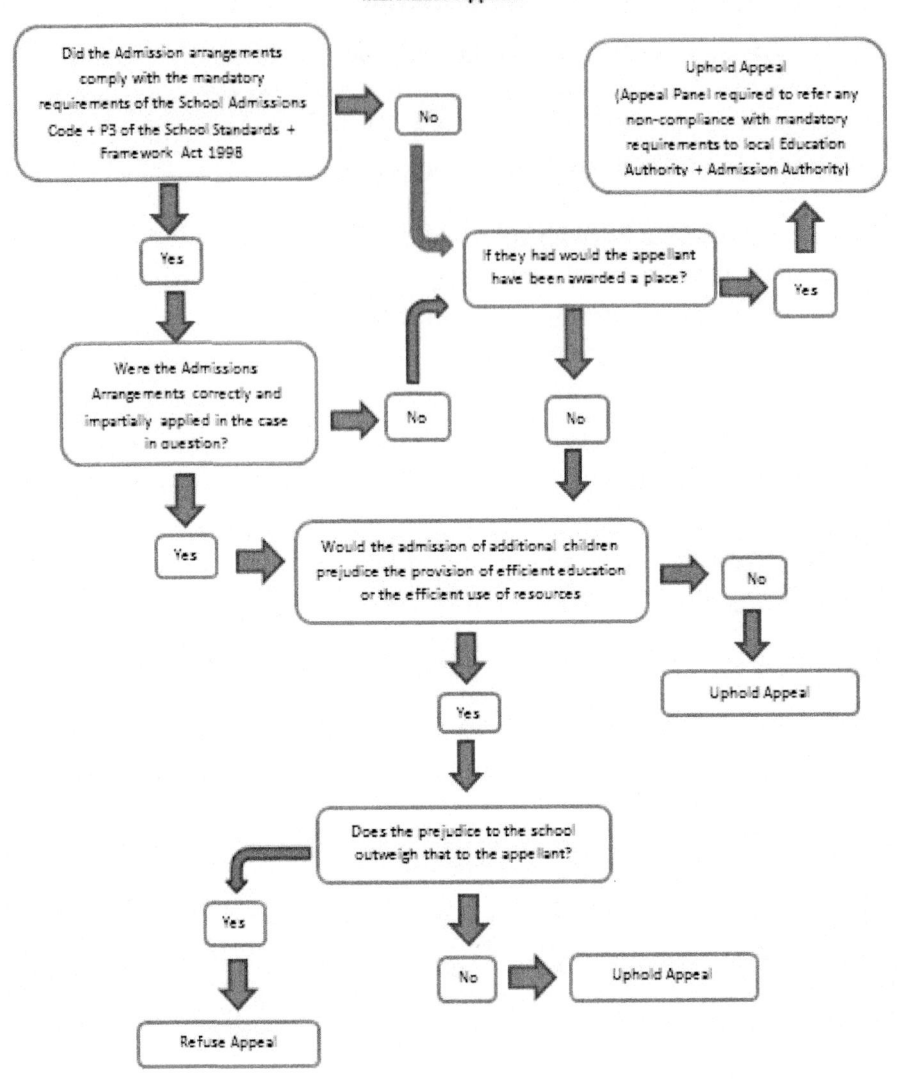

```
┌─────────────────────────────┐
│ Did the Admission           │
│ arrangements comply with    │──No──┐
│ the mandatory requirements  │      │
│ of the School Admissions    │      │
│ Code + P3 of the School     │      │
│ Standards + Framework       │      │
│ Act 1998                    │      │
└──────────┬──────────────────┘      │
           │                         ▼
          Yes              ┌──────────────────────┐      ┌─────────────────────────────┐
           │               │ If they had would    │      │ Uphold Appeal               │
           ▼               │ the appellant have   │──Yes→│ (Appeal Panel required to   │
┌─────────────────────┐    │ been awarded a place?│      │ refer any non-compliance    │
│ Were the Admissions │    └──────────┬───────────┘      │ with mandatory requirements │
│ Arrangements        │──No──┐        │                  │ to local Education          │
│ correctly and       │      │       No                  │ Authority + Admission       │
│ impartially applied │      │        │                  │ Authority)                  │
│ in the case in      │      │        ▼                  └─────────────────────────────┘
│ question?           │      │
└──────────┬──────────┘      │
           │                 │
          Yes                │
           │                 ▼
           │       ┌──────────────────────────────────────┐
           └──────→│ Would the admission of additional    │──No──┐
                   │ children prejudice the provision of  │      │
                   │ efficient education or the efficient │      ▼
                   │ use of resources                     │   ┌───────────────┐
                   └──────────┬───────────────────────────┘   │ Uphold Appeal │
                              │                               └───────────────┘
                             Yes
                              │
                              ▼
                   ┌──────────────────────────────┐
                   │ Does the prejudice to the    │
                   │ school outweigh that to the  │
                   │ appellant?                   │
                   └──┬────────────────────┬──────┘
                     Yes                  No───→┌───────────────┐
                      │                         │ Uphold Appeal │
                      ▼                         └───────────────┘
               ┌───────────────┐
               │ Refuse Appeal │
               └───────────────┘
```

The decision making process followed by the Appeal Panel has two stages.

First Stage- examining the decision to refuse admission to the child

The School Admission Appeals Code 2012 states that the following matters must be considered by the Appeal Panel in relation to each child that is the subject of an appeal:

"a). whether the admission arrangements (including the area's co-ordinated admission arrangements) complied with the mandatory requirements of the School Admissions Code and Part 3 of the School Standards and Framework Act 1998; and

b). whether the admission arrangements were correctly and impartially applied in the case in question."

Compliance with mandatory requirements

Admission Authorities are required to comply with certain requirements in relation to the School Admissions Code in terms of their Admission Arrangements. These include prescribed consultation periods. See Appendix B for full details of the relevant section of the School Admissions Code.

The Admission Authority is required to provide details of how it has complied with the mandatory requirements, and how the admission arrangements and co-ordinated admissions scheme apply to the appellant's application in the evidence that is sent out to all parties in advance of the Appeal.

Correct and impartial application of the admission arrangements

The Admission Authority is required to demonstrate that the admission arrangements were applied correctly in relation to the appellant. Examples of information that could be provided by the Admission Authority to do this include:

If the Appeal Panel "finds that the Admission Arrangements did not comply with admissions law or had not been correctly and impartially applied, and the child would have been offered a place if the arrangements had complied or had been correctly and impartially applied", the Appeal must be upheld. It is important to emphasise that where it is found that the Admissions Arrangements haven't been correctly applied, the Appeal Panel have to be satisfied that the error resulted in the child not being offered a place at the school that they would have been offered had the Admission Arrangements been applied correctly. If they found that there had been a mistake in the application of the Admission Arrangements but that the child wouldn't have been allocated a place if they had been done correctly, they would not be required to uphold the Appeal.

The School Admission Appeals Code then states "that the panel must then decide whether the admission of additional children would prejudice the provision of efficient education or the efficient use of resources". In Admissions, "prejudice" is taken to mean causing detriment to the ability of staff to manage and for children to receive the best education. An additional child being admitted could cause this due to overcrowding, dilution of teacher: staff ratios which reduce the ability and time of staff to support pupils individually and the general erosion of standards at the school because of this.

This means that the school in addition to stating that they have reached their Published Admission Number in the relevant year group (the year group for which the appellant is appealing for a place) has to demonstrate how additional children would cause prejudice to the efficient education or efficient use of resources.

Examples of information that the Admission Authority could provide to demonstrate this could include mentioning overcrowding problems with the physical school facilities, the impact of additional children on staffing resources and the increase in teaching group size. Detailed examples are provided later in this book.

These points make the case of the Admission Authority for the Appeal Hearing.

The School Admission Appeals Code 2012 states that the Appeal Panel must uphold (grant) the appeal at the first stage where:

"a). It finds that the admission arrangements did not comply with admissions law or had not been correctly and impartially applied, and the child would have been offered a place if the arrangements had complied or had been correctly and impartially applied; or

b). it finds that the admission of additional children <u>would not</u> prejudice the provision of efficient education or efficient use of resources"

The only exception to this is for a multiple group of appeals to the same year group (usually for Reception or Year 7 intakes) where if a number of children would have their appeals granted at this point, and to admit that number would seriously prejudice the provision of efficient education or efficient use of resources, the panel is required to proceed to the second stage.

The School Admission Appeals Code 2012 states that the panel must proceed to the second stage where:

"a). it finds that the admission arrangements did comply with admissions law and that they were correctly and impartially applied to the child; or

b) it finds that the admission arrangements did not comply with admissions law or were not correctly and impartially applied but that, if they had complied and had been correctly and impartially applied, the child would not have been offered a place; and it finds that the admission of additional children <u>would</u> prejudice the provision of efficient education or efficient use of resources"

Second stage- balancing the arguments

The next stage of the Appeal is where the appellant states their reasons for wishing their child to be granted a place at the school being appealed for.

The Appeal Panel is required to balance the prejudice to the school (in taking an additional child) against the appellant's case for the child to be admitted to the school (i.e. prejudice to the child if they aren't granted a place). The Panel has to take into consideration the appellant's reasons for expressing a preference for that school, including what that specific school can offer the child that the allocated, or other schools cannot. If the panel considers that the appellant's case outweighs the school's case then it must uphold the appeal.

When considering prejudice, the Admission Authority must be able to demonstrate prejudice over and above the fact that the published admission number has already been reached. The Appeal Panel cannot reassess the capacity of the school, but has to consider the impact on the school of any additional children being admitted. In deciding if there would be prejudice or not, the Appeal Panel may consider the following factors

a). what effect an additional child would have on the school in the current and following academic years as that year group moves up through the school;

b). whether the school's physical accommodation or organisation has had any changes since the admission number was originally set for the relevant year group;

c). the impact of the locally agreed Fair Access Protocol

d). the impact on the organisation and size of classes, the availability of teaching staff and the effect on children already attending the school if an additional child was admitted.

For multiple appeals, the Appeal Panel must not compare the individual cases when deciding if an appellant's case outweighs the prejudice to the school unless it finds that there are more cases which outweigh prejudice than the school can admit, then it will compare the cases and uphold those with the strongest cases for admission. Where a certain number of children could be admitted without causing prejudice, the panel must uphold the appeals of at least that number of children. The Appeal Panel must be consistent in its decision making.

All decisions made by the Appeal Panel are binding on the school. Appeal Panels cannot make decisions with any form of conditions or future requirements (such as if the child attained certain grades or attendance levels), they have to make them at the conclusion of the Appeals being heard in that year group for that school.

Class Size Legislation Appeals

Appeals which come under Class Size Legislation are different because the Appeal Panel only has certain set reasons for which it can grant the Appeal to the appellant.

In summary, the only reasons that a Class Size Legislation appeal can be granted are:

- The child would have been offered a place if the admission arrangements had complied with the relevant legislation
- The child would have been offered a place if the admission arrangements had been applied correctly
- The Appeal Panel finds that the decision to refuse admission to the child was not one that a reasonable authority would have made in the circumstances of the case.

The information below is for appeals where an Admission Authority has refused to grant a place to a child on the grounds that the admission of a further child would breach the infant class size limit and there are no measures it could take to avoid this without prejudicing the provision of efficient education or efficient use of resources. Decisions on appeals for infant classes where the refusal was for any other reason are dealt with in the manner outlined above.

As before, the Appeal Panel has to follow a two stage process in making the decision as to whether it will uphold the Appeal.

First stage- examining the decision to refuse admission

The Appeal Panel has to consider all of the points listed below as listed in the School Admission Appeals Code 2012:

"a). whether the admission of an additional child / additional children would breach the infant class size limit;

b). whether the admission arrangements (including the area's co-ordinated admission arrangements) complied with the mandatory requirements of the School Admissions Code and Part 3 of the School Standards and Framework Act 1998;

c). whether the admission arrangements were correctly and impartially applied in the case(s) in question; and

d). whether the decision to refuse admission was one which a reasonable admission authority would have made in the circumstances of the case"

The Appeal Panel is <u>only</u> allowed to uphold the Appeal at this stage where:

"a). It finds that the admission of additional children would not breach the infant class size limit; or

b). it finds that the admission arrangements did not comply with admissions law or were not correctly and impartially applied and the child would have been offered a place if the arrangements had complied or had been correctly and impartially applied; or

c). it decides that the decision to refuse admission was not one which a reasonable admission authority would have made in the circumstances of the case"

The Appeal Panel must refuse the appeal after the first stage if it finds that:

"a). it finds that the admissions arrangements did comply with admissions law and were correctly and impartially applied; or

b). it finds that the admission arrangements did not comply with admissions law or were not correctly or impartially applied, but that, if they had complied and had been correctly and impartially applied, the child would not have been offered a place;

and it finds that the decision to refuse admission was one which a reasonable admission authority could have made"

These are the only grounds on which a Class Size Legislation Appeal can be granted.

Similarly to other appeals, if for multiple appeals, a number of children would have been offered a place following the first stage (such as if the admission arrangements had been done incorrectly), and to admit that number of children would seriously prejudice the provision of efficient education or efficient use of resources, the panel have to go onto the second stage.

Second stage- comparing cases

The Appeal Panel has to compare the appellants' cases for their children to be admitted and decide which to uphold. If the school could admit a certain number of children without breaching the infant class size limit (or without needing to take measures to avoid breaching it that would prejudice the provision of efficient education or efficient use of resources) the panel _must_ uphold the appeals of at least that number of children.

Reasonableness when used in the legislation applying to School Admission Appeals has a specific definition and the threshold is high. For the Appeal Panel to find that the decision was not one that a reasonable authority would make, they need to be satisfied that the decision to refuse to admit the child was "perverse in the light of the admission arrangements" , so "beyond the range of responses open to a reasonable decision maker" or "a decision which is so outrageous in its defiance of logic or of accepted moral standards that no sensible person who had applied his mind to the question could have arrived at it".

5 SO YOU WANT TO APPEAL- WHAT HAPPENS NOW?

Summary

If you have decided you would like to Appeal, you will need to inform the Admission Authority of this. You will then receive a letter notifying you of the date and time of the Appeal.

If asked to in the letter, you should contact the Admission Authority or Clerk to inform them if you will be able to attend the Appeal on the date and time you have been given.

If you can't attend on the date and time given, you may be able to get the Appeal rearranged within the Appeals being held for that school if they are over several days, or you could have it heard without you being there, or you could ask the Admission Authority if it could be arranged for another date although if this is possible it could be quite some time after the original date you were given.

Notifying the Admission Authority that you wish to Appeal

If you have decided that you would like to Appeal, you need to inform the Admission Authority. The letter that informed you that you had not been offered a place at the school should state that you have the right to appeal the decision, and give details of how to lodge an Appeal.

You may have to telephone to ask for an Appeal Form to be sent out to you, or you might be able to download it off their website. The refusal letter should state the deadline for lodging an Appeal.

It is important to submit your Appeal Form within the deadline for these appeals as if you are very late in submitting your Appeal request for Reception and Year 7 in the normal Admission Round, it may not be dealt with until after the Summer Holidays. Although the Admission Authority is required to hold appeals for the normal admission round (Reception / Year 7) that have been lodged by their deadline within 40 school days, the time is measured in school days. This means the time does not include school holidays or weekends, so it can be quite a long time depending on how the Easter holidays fall in relation to the deadline given by the Admission Authority. So if an application is late, although the School Admission Code states that applications should be held within 40 school days of the deadline where possible, or within 30 school days of the appeal being lodged, if it is a very late application it could be that the deadline falls after the Summer Holidays.

You can submit additional information and evidence with your Appeal form if you wish, or submit it once you have been notified of the Appeal date and the deadline for the submission of further information.

<u>Invitation letter</u>

Once you have submitted your Appeal form, it can take a while for all the Appeal applications to be processed by the Admission

Authority and for an appeal date to be scheduled. Notification of the Appeal date and time must be provided in writing. Admission Authorities must provide the invitation letter no later than 10 school days before the date of the Appeal.

Parents can waive their right to 10 school days' notice of the hearing if they wish. This can allow their Appeal to be heard more quickly if their application for an Appeal arrives after invitation letters have been sent out for a particular Appeal date which has space for an additional Appeal hearing, or to take advantage of a cancellation.

The invitation letter must provide details of the Appeal date, time and location. It must also provide a deadline by which any additional evidence or information needs to be submitted, and inform appellants that information provided after this date may not be considered at the Appeal hearing. The Admission Authority must also ask appellants if they plan to call any witnesses or be represented at the hearing. If the invitation letter asks you to contact the Admission Authority or Clerk to confirm that you are attending your appeal, it is important to do this.

What if I cannot attend on the given date?

If it is not possible to attend on the date given for the Appeal Hearing, it is important to contact the Clerk to the Appeal to inform them of this as soon as possible. They will be able to give the options available to you. In many cases, the Admission Authority would try to offer an alternative date. For multiple appeals over several days (in the usual admission round) it may be possible to move the Appeal hearing to another of those dates. If it is a single day of Appeals, the Clerk and Admission Authority are likely to be able to defer the Appeal to another, later date, but it is worth bearing in mind that this could be a few weeks later than the original Appeal date given. If the original Appeal date offered is within the required timescales, the Admission Authority has fulfilled its duty in complying with these timescales. In many cases, any Appeals that have been rearranged will be added to another Appeal date that is already scheduled, if there is space, or a day can be scheduled for all the outstanding Appeals heard.

If an appellant prefers, instead of asking that their appeal be deferred, they can either send another person (e.g. friend or family member) to attend and represent them, or they can ask that the Appeal be heard in their absence. When an Appeal is heard in absence, the Appeal Panel uses the written information that the appellant has provided to determine the Appeal outcome. If the appellant wishes to send another person to represent them at the Appeal, they are often asked to confirm this in writing in advance of the Appeal.

If an appellant has previously informed the Clerk that they will be attending, but then fails to turn up for the Appeal hearing, it is common practice to give a small amount of extra time but if they still have not made contact or turned up the Appeal will usually be held in their absence.

6 PREPARING FOR YOUR APPEAL- SUBMITTING EVIDENCE

Summary

The letter that notifies you of your Appeal Hearing date and time should give details of how to submit additional evidence, and the deadline that you need to submit it by.

When thinking about what evidence you may wish to submit, consider why you need your child to go to the school that the Appeal is for. Then think if there is any evidence that you could provide to prove the reasons for wanting your child to go to that school.

It is important to submit the evidence by the deadline given, as this allows it to be circulated to the Appeal Panel members in advance of the Appeal. They can then read it before the Appeal. The Appeal Panel members do not have to accept evidence at the Appeal itself, although they may allow single letters they would be reluctant to accept large quantities of information as it is likely that the Appeal would have to be adjourned to allow them to read it.

Preparing for your Appeal

Once your Appeal date is known, it is a good idea to begin to prepare for the Appeal hearing if you haven't before.

Submitting further evidence

The invitation letter will state the deadline for submitting further evidence in advance of the Appeal. Although many Appeal Panels will accept a small amount of evidence at the hearing itself (such as a single letter) they are allowed to refuse to accept further evidence on the day. This is to prevent appellants submitting large amounts of additional information that would require the Appeal to be adjourned in order for Appeal Panel to read it. This would be detrimental to the smooth running of the Appeals on the day as the subsequent Appeal hearings would then be delayed. Therefore it is advisable to submit any evidence in advance of the Appeal hearing, in time for the deadline given. This is to allow the Clerk to send out all of the evidence relating to each Appeal to all the parties concerned (Presenting Officer and Appeal Panel Members). The Clerk will also send a copy of the Admission Authority's case out to the appellants in advance of the Appeal. Previous legislation stated that this had to be done 7 days in advance of the hearing but this has now been changed to "a reasonable time before the hearing", so all parties should receive all the relevant information far enough ahead of the Appeal date to allow them to read it beforehand.

Think about why you want your child to attend this particular school. If there are any reasons that you could provide evidence for, collect the evidence and send it so that it arrives prior to the deadline.

If you are intending on telling the Appeal Panel that your child should have been given a place but an error on the part of the Admission Authority prevented this, think about what you could provide as evidence. The more evidence that can be given that proves the application was made correctly and on time the stronger your case. It would be much more difficult to convince an Appeal Panel that an error was made by the Admission Authority by losing an application in some way without providing proof that they received it in the first place.

Reason	Possible evidence
Application was done online on time and completed	Screenshots of application process Screenshot / print out of email acknowledging application completed and submitted
Application was sent in by post on time	Recorded delivery / tracking proof that the application was received by the Admission

	Authority Some Admission Authorities provide a postcard that can be sent out to confirm receipt of application- if this is available this makes excellent evidence of the Admission Authority having received the application and the date that it was received.

Bear in mind that you are asking an Appeal Panel to add a child to a school that is already full, so the more relevant evidence that can help strengthen your case the better. Remember that you are appealing to get into the school for which the Appeal is for, rather than out of the school allocated. This is important as you need to provide a compelling argument as to why your child needs to attend this particular school rather than any others that may have places available. You may have more than one reason to wish your child to attend the school, you can submit evidence if you have it for all of your reasons.

Examples of possible reasons that could be evidenced are given below:

Reason	Possible evidence
Child has aptitude for a particular sport that this school offers that the allocated school does not. Perhaps the child is successfully competing in this sport and is considering taking this further in the future with more competitions.	Proof from sport club or other qualified person stating the child's aptitude for the sport and their potential future success if they did have the opportunity to continue with it at this school. Proof that the allocated school doesn't offer this sport.

Child is being bullied at existing school and this has been reported to the school and or police	Any letters or emails between the appellant and the school which would confirm that bullying had been reported and any other relevant information such as the action taken by the school to address the issue. Letter from police confirming this, with any additional information they are willing to provide. Doctor or other relevant professional's letter stating the effect of the bullying on the child.
Child has a favourite subject that they wish to study for the future and are particularly good at that is not offered at the school at which they have been allocated a place and the school they are appealing for does offer it / has it as a specialist subject	Letter from the current school confirming the child's aptitude and enthusiasm for this particular subject

Allocated school has no direct bus routes so travelling time is excessive, whereas the school appealed for has a direct bus route which would mean the child didn't have to spend x time travelling every day and leaving at x time in the morning / getting home at x time at night at x age, particularly in winter when it is dark. Could also state that child has no friends from their area travelling to that school so they would have to do the journey on their own which would be particularly concerning in the winter months.	Proof of bus routes, for both schools if the comparison between them is relevant to the appellant's case
Affordability of travel to school	If affordability of the child's travel to school is an issue, proof of the costs between the allocated school and the school appealing for could be provided to demonstrate the difference in costs.
Family has just moved house and it is no longer possible for child to attend old school due to the move	Proof that family has moved house- tenancy agreement for new house / final utility bill for last house. If an appellant's case is that they have moved house and are now very close to the school they really need to provide proof that they are now residing at the new address or the Appeal Panel may not take it into account.

Child was living with one parent but this arrangement has now changed and they have moved in with the other parent or family member and attending previous school is no longer possible	Written confirmation of the child's move. Letter from parent who the child lived with previously stating that the child no longer lives with them. Proof that the child benefit if any is being paid to the parent the child now lives with can help provide proof that the move to the other parent is intended to be long term. If there are any issues which might affect the child in relation to the circumstances of the move (such as a relationship breakdown or bereavement), it may be advisable to provide further information and any supporting evidence / letters that relate to this and perhaps demonstrate why this child in particular needs to go to this particular school.
Child or parent have medical conditions which the appellant feels means that they need to attend the school that they are appealing for	Confirmation of the medical condition from doctor or other relevant professional and how it impacts on the child / family resulting in the child needing to attend this school.
Other family members attend the school and the appellant wishes their child to attend the same school for support / childcare / other reasons	Confirmation of the other family members attending the school. Particularly those living in the same house such as step siblings etc.

Relationship breakdown between the child's parents resulting in a need to change school, perhaps due to a house move	Legal documents could be used to confirm this together with proof of the move.
Allocated school does not have an afterschool club or other childcare provision, the school appealed for does and the parent feels that their working hours mean that they have to be able to access the additional childcare at the school	Proof of the appellant's working hours such as letter from their employer stating the hours and also if they would not be willing to change them to accommodate school pick up and drop offs. Proof that the allocated school does not offer the childcare required
Existing Child-minder does not cover the allocated school.	Letter from the existing child-minder. This alone is unlikely to be sufficient to convince the Panel, but if the appellant has found there are no child-minders that will cover the school available and can prove this, that may strengthen their case more than just a letter from the existing child-minder.

Child is a looked after or previously looked after child.	Documents proving that the child is either currently looked after or a previously looked after child. Also if the Admission Authority was informed of this as part of the application, proof that they were provided with this information such as a copy of the application / screenshots.
Child needs to attend this school for religious reasons.	Proof as appropriate to the school. E.g. Letter from vicar confirming church attendance including how long and how often. E.g. Certificate of baptism

Remember that an Appeal Panel has to make a decision using the information and evidence available to it on the day. Supporting information or evidence cannot be provided after the Appeals have concluded as the decisions will have been made. Therefore it needs to be submitted in advance of the hearing. It is at the Appeal Panel's discretion whether they will accept additional evidence at the Appeal itself so to be sure that it can be used it needs to be submitted by the deadline given in the invitation letter.

It is a good idea to have a copy of the information that you have submitted to bring to the Appeal so that you can refer to it if needed.

7 PREPARING FOR YOUR APPEAL- THE ADMISSION AUTHORITY'S CASE

Summary

You will receive the Admission Authority's Case prior to the Appeal. It should arrive early enough so that you get a few days before the Appeal to read it.

The Admission Authority's Case will detail why it was not possible for your child to be allocated a place at the School which you are appealing for. It will also specify how the Admission Arrangements comply with the legislation.

The Case will also state that "the admission of additional children would prejudice the provision of efficient education or the efficient use of resources" and will go on to give reasons for this. Reasons can include overcrowding, reduction in teacher time and increasing of group sizes. The reasons given will vary for each school.

The Admission Authority's Case

A week or so before the Appeal date, you will be sent the Admission Authority's case (sometimes called the Statement Of Case). This document sets out the Admission Authority's case with respect to your Appeal.

Firstly, they will seek to demonstrate that the Admission Arrangements complied with the relevant legislation, and that they were applied correctly to the appellant.

Some examples of what information could be given, either in the information sent out in advance, or in the case made by the Presenting Officer at the Appeal itself are below:

- Details regarding the number of children admitted from each oversubscription criteria together with clarification of the criteria in which the appellant was placed. This could be used to demonstrate that the places were allocated in line with the oversubscription criteria, and that the appellant was refused a place because all places were allocated to children in higher criteria (such as if children with siblings at the school were given a higher criteria, and all places were allocated to children in that and higher criteria, but the appellant did not have a sibling at the school so had a lower criteria).
- The Presenting Officer will often state that the decision not to admit the appellant's child was not personal, and that their application was dealt with in line with their Admissions Policy.
- Cut off distance- this would be relevant in many appeals where distance was used to rank applications as part of the admission arrangements. The cut off distance is the distance that the last child offered a place at the school lives from the school. A cut off distance would be provided and used to demonstrate the correct application of the admission arrangements by also stating the distance of each appellant from the school. This would demonstrate

that the appellant was refused a place at the school because they lived further away than the cut off distance, i.e. that all the places had been allocated to children living closer to the school than the applicant.
- Date of application- if an application for a school place is made after the deadline, it can result in a child who is of a higher oversubscription criteria than others who were allocated a place being refused one. This can happen because when the allocation of places is done, the places are allocated to applicants who have applied by that date in line with the oversubscription criteria. If an application is received after this time, even if the applicant would fall into a higher oversubscription criteria than some of the children who were allocated places, they would not receive a place because they would have all been allocated to on time applications i.e. by the time the application was received there were no places left to allocate. In this type of case, the evidence sent out by the Admission Authority and the Presenting Officer's case would seek to demonstrate how the places were allocated to on time applicants and how there were no places left by the time the appellant's application was made. This is more relevant to appeals in the usual admission round i.e. Reception and Year 7 places.
- Numbers of pupils in the school and relevant year group- this is more relevant to In-year appeals. The Admission Authority would give details of how many children were in the relevant year group, if there had been no spaces available since the appellant had applied for the place due to the numbers reaching or exceeding the Published Admission Number that would show that the Admission Arrangements had been applied correctly as there had not been a place available since the time of application. If a place had been available at any point since the application was made, the Admission Authority would need to show that the Admission Arrangements had been applied

correctly in this situation by giving details of the oversubscription criteria of the appellant and the child who had been allocated the place who would, if done correctly, have been in a higher oversubscription criteria.

The Presenting Officer will then try to demonstrate that "the admission of additional children would prejudice the provision of efficient education or the efficient use of resources".

Some examples of what information could be given, either in the information sent out in advance, or in the case made by the Presenting Officer at the Appeal itself are below:

- The school was built many years ago and designed for less children than it has now as the school has expanded over the years. Whilst teaching areas have been added to by converting existing space within the school, and extending the building, the internal corridors remain the same. Because they were designed for less children than the school has currently, there are issues around traffic and congestion in the corridors particularly at lesson change over times. This creates Health and Safety concerns, particularly for the smaller children. Some schools might have implemented a one way system to try to increase safety but the addition of further children to the school would still increase the problems with corridors.
- Toilet provision and changing areas are also often used as examples to demonstrate why the school could not admit any additional children. Sometimes schools have increased their numbers over the years but have not increased toilet or changing room provision, and schools that have converted non-teaching space into additional space have often used changing rooms resulting in insufficient provision of these facilities.
- The size of classrooms, particularly in newer schools which are designed specifically for no more than 30 children in a class. Some schools have classrooms which only have 30

desks and chairs for each classroom, and there is not room in them to add another set of furniture for an additional child due to the restrictive design of the classrooms. Lack of room and ability to change the layout or classroom design is also a problem that can affect schools in very old buildings, particularly if they are listed as this creates additional limitations to their ability to make changes.
- Children are often grouped in terms of ability, with larger groups for the higher ability children to allow for smaller group sizes for children who need more help, and the provision of one to one teaching support for children with additional needs. The addition of another child would either mean adding to an already large group or increasing the size of the smaller groups, both of which would mean diluting the teaching provision available to existing children at the school. Increasing the number of children would increase the demands on teaching provision, reducing the ability to provide small study groups and one to one teaching support as needed. This would be prejudicial to the children already at the school.
- Additional numbers of children at the school would increase the demand on pastoral support staff, reducing their ability to provide the support needed to children on an individual basis.
- Technical subjects such as chemistry and biology often need smaller group sizes in order for children to be able to do the practical work themselves. Larger group sizes can either mean that children have to share rather than do the work individually which changes the learning experience for both of the children. In some cases, large group sizes can cause Health and Safety issues in relation to space available in the technical rooms, meaning that instead of doing the practical themselves, they have to watch the teacher demonstrate it to them. This could particularly apply for practical work involving flames where it would

not be safe to have children doing it if there were too many in the room.
- Other practical subjects such as textiles require teachers to give individual attention to pupils, and their ability to do this is decreased with larger group sizes. Adding further children would exacerbate this.
- ICT is another subject which is often designed to have no more than 30 children in a group. ICT rooms have 30 computers, and the addition of another child would result in two children having to share. This would alter the learning experience for at least one existing child in the year group of the appellant's child should they be admitted.
- Larger group sizes resulting in overcrowding reduce the ability of teaching staff to be flexible in their teaching methods, particularly when rooms are overcrowded and movement is difficult because of this. This, along with the reduction in the teacher's ability to offer individual feedback and support has a detrimental effect on the teaching provision and learning experience.
- Information is often provided about the high level of additional need of existing pupils in the school. This is particularly relevant in the case of In-Year appeals where information can be provided about that year group. There may be a breakdown of the number of children with additional needs in that year group, what particular facilities and teaching methods have to be provided for them and any additional teaching support that is required.

For example if a school has a high number of children with additional needs, they may be providing small group sessions or more individual support which reduces their ability to accommodate further children as the resources are already stretched. If pupils have a teaching assistant with them as support throughout the school day, as well as the impact on the staffing requirements of the school,

- there is the physical impact of another adult in the classroom, exacerbating any overcrowding issues.
- Presenting Officers will often state that schools are incentivised to take as many children as possible because the more children they have the more funding they receive. However they have to balance this with the ability to continue to deliver the national curriculum to the same high standards as they are currently. The addition of further children would erode these standards due to overcrowding and stretching of resources.

Once you have the Admission Authority's case, try to think about if you can try to disprove it. If you are alleging that an error was made in the allocations process and your child should have been offered a place in the allocation of places, you will need to be able to convince the Appeal Panel that this is the case. Any evidence such as proof of postage / delivery of the application form, print off of confirmation email for an online application need to be brought to the appeal as well as being submitted as part of your additional evidence. This will allow you to refer to them when you are presenting your case.

If you believe that the School does have capacity to accept additional children without causing prejudice to the school, think about why you believe this. Can you provide any proof? Perhaps you know that building work has started at the school which you think will increase their capacity, or that a pupil has just left and another pupil has not been allocated a place at the school. Maybe you have looked at the staffing lists at the school and it appears that there is enough teaching staff to allow for more children to be there. You might be aware that the school has previously had significantly more children than it's Published Admission Number in that year.

The Admission Authority has to comply with reasonable requests from appellants for information which they need to prepare for their appeals, such information could include details of the numbers of children in the year group, the Published Admission Number for that year group, numbers of children admitted into that year in previous years, numbers of children accepted on Appeal in previous years (this does not mean that an Appeal Panel would automatically admit that number again as they do not have quotas, but it could help demonstrate that the school could cope with more children than their Published Admission Number if it has done so before), details of pupil migration i.e. numbers of children leaving and joining the school.

Once you have all the information you need about to the School's Case, it is worth collating it all and making notes on the points you wish to raise at the Appeal hearing, both as questions and as part of making your case. Possible questions that may be useful to ask are detailed below.

<u>Questions to ask the Admission Authority</u>

- What was the criteria and cut off distance for the last child to be allocated a place?
    - If the last child allocated a place was of a lower criteria or the same criteria as your child but further away, you can then ask for further information to clarify the situation such as making sure your child was treated as an on time application if you applied on time. You could provide proof of your application if available.
- -How many children were accepted into the year group last year? (for Reception or Year 7 appeals).
    - If more than the Published Admission Number- did the school choose to take them or were the extra children a result of successful Appeals? How did they cope with the additional children? If the school chose to take the additional children why are they not taking extra this year? How did they cope with the increased number of children?

- What is pupil movement at the school like- is there a high turnover or little movement?
- Are there any plans to expand the school?
- For in year appeals- what is the maximum number of children that have been in this year group? How did the school cope with that number of children? When did they leave? If they coped with that number of children previously why can't they cope with them now?

The Appeal Panel will also ask the Presenting Officers questions. They are likely to ask for clarification that the admissions arrangements comply with legislation as well as other questions relating to the School's Case. If a Presenting Officer does not have the information to hand to answer the question, the Appeal Panel can adjourn the meeting to allow the Presenting Officer to find out the information. If this happens, you would be asked to leave the room as neither the appellant or the Presenting Officer is allowed to be alone with the Appeal Panel. The Clerk would then ask everyone to come back into the room once the Presenting Officer had the necessary information and the Appeal Hearing could continue.

8 PREPARING FOR YOUR APPEAL- YOUR CASE

Summary

Before your Appeal, you should think about why you want / need your child to go to the school which you are appealing for. You will have started to think about this when you were deciding what evidence to submit in advance.

Remember that you are trying to convince the Appeal Panel that your child needs to be given a place in a school which is already full, so your argument needs to be compelling.

Your Case

You need to try your best to convince the Appeal Panel that it would be less prejudicial to the school to have to admit an additional child than it would be prejudicial to your child if they were not allowed a place at the school. Remember you are not appealing to get out of the allocated school as such, you are appealing to convince the Appeal Panel to allow an extra child into a school which is already full when there might be places available in other schools in the area. Therefore the more compelling your case for this particular school, the better your chance of convincing the Appeal Panel.

Sometimes, Presenting Officers will have details of schools in the area with places available in the relevant year group which they will mention in their presentation. This is intended to strengthen the School's case with respect to not adding an extra child to a school which is already full when there are other places available elsewhere. It is worth contacting the Local Education Authority in the day or two before the Appeal to find out what places are available so that if the Presenting Officer makes reference to the schools with places you will have had the chance to formulate arguments as to why those schools are not suitable but the school you are appealing for is.

Think about why you feel your child should attend that school specifically. You will have started to think about this when you were considering what additional evidence to submit but go over it again in case you come up with more reasons and make a list. Possible reasons could include:

-The school you are appealing for is very close to where you live. This would be much more convenient in terms of getting your child to school, perhaps you don't drive and your child would have to walk to school which would be impossible for the allocated school due to it being further away. If you have to walk your child to school perhaps you have other, smaller, children who would struggle to walk that distance twice a day (drop off and pick up- there and back). Perhaps the allocated school is so far away that travel times mean it would be impossible for them to do any after school clubs or socialise with other pupils out of school, but if they attended the school you are appealing for they could access all the clubs and socialise with the other children out of school as many come from the area in which you live. You would be worried about your child being isolated from their local peer group if they couldn't attend the same school as them.

- Why, specifically, does your child need to attend this school in your opinion? Perhaps they are a specialist in a particular subject that your child is gifted in or intends to pursue as a future career. Perhaps your child excels at a particular sport and this school offers far more opportunity to continue with and progress in the sport.

- Does your child have a medical condition that you feel means they need to attend the school you are appealing for? Or perhaps someone who looks after the child has a medical condition that means they need them to attend that school.

- Will all your child's friends be attending the school? Do they have difficulty making new friends? Why would it be better for them to go to a school with their existing friends rather than go to a school where they would need to make new friends?

- Does your childcare depend on your child attending the school you are appealing for? Maybe you have a sharing arrangement with a neighbour or the child minder only picks up from that school or that school offers wrap around childcare but the school you have been allocated does not. Do your working times mean that you would find it very difficult to drop off / pick up from the allocated school?

- Does your child already have a sibling or other family member attending the school you are appealing for? Check the school's

Admission Policy for their definition of "sibling". Why do you want them to go to the same school as their sibling? Will the sibling provide support for the child there/ make it easier to get them both to the same school rather than having to get children to different schools / the child that you are appealing for wants to go to school with their sibling or other family member.

- If you have just moved into the area, think about how the move is relevant to your Appeal. Why did you move into the area? Is attending that particular school (if it is near to your home) important to your child in terms of letting them integrate into their local community by making friends nearby? If the house move was due to a relationship breakdown, either between the child's parents or between the child and their other parent how has this affected the child? How would getting them into this school help them deal with this situation?

- Are you wanting to change school because your child has experienced bullying in their last / current school? If in the current school, how severe has it been (give examples), how have the school dealt with it, has it been going on for a long time, has the situation been resolved, how has it affected your child, were the police involved? Maybe you are appealing for Secondary School but you are worried about your child attending the allocated school because you know that children who have been causing your child great distress through bullying will be attending the allocated school but not the one being appealed for.

- If the allocated school is a distance away and involves a significant journey to school, you might be worried about them having to do this journey on their own. Perhaps it involves more than one bus and extended time waiting at bus stops which is a particular worry in winter with the dark nights in terms of your child's safety. You might also have found that your child would have to leave the house very early and get back late in the afternoon evening because of the travel time involved and you worry about the impact this would have on them in terms of tiredness, lack of time to do homework or access any after school clubs.

- Do you particularly want your child to attend the school you are attending for religious reasons? Maybe the allocated school is a faith school. Whatever your reasons, think them through so that you can give the Appeal Panel full details at the hearing.

Please note that the examples above are purely examples and not an exhaustive list. You will have your own reasons for wanting your child to attend the school you are appealing for. It is also very important to note that it is up to the Appeal Panel to evaluate the case put forward by each appellant as part of their decision making process and determine how much weight they put on different reasons given in balancing the School's and appellant's cases. Unfortunately there isn't a way to guarantee to win an Appeal, but the more reasons put forward to strengthen your case, the better your chance of having your Appeal granted. The list above is to demonstrate how you might want to think about the case you wanted to put forward as the more information you can provide the Appeal Panel on the day, the better your chance of convincing them that your child should go to the school you are appealing for.

It is worth writing your reasons down so that you have them to refer to in the Appeal. There is nothing wrong with having bullet points or notes with you to remind you of the points you wish to make, or questions you wish to ask at the Appeal hearing. Many parents find it very helpful to have written down their key points and questions beforehand so that they do not worry about forgetting to say something.

Questions asked by the Appeal Panel and Presenting Officer

The Appeal Panel will ask you questions about what you have said, and the Presenting Officer is also allowed to ask you questions if they wish. Questions often relate to the information you have submitted in advance of the Appeal as well as what you said on the day. Some example questions are listed below to give you an idea of the type of questions that can be asked:

- Following a house move- Why have you moved and is the move intended to be permanent?
- Does your child want to go to the school that you are appealing for? What do they think about this situation?
- Have you visited the school you are appealing for? What did you think?
- Have you visited the school that you have been allocated?
- How would your child get to school? – for the allocated school and the school being appealed for. Is there anyone who could help you with getting your child to school?
- For bullying cases- What has the current school done to address the issues? How successful have they been? If your child moved school do you think the bullying issue would recur again? How would you deal with that and how does the school you want to go to deal with bullying?
- Was this school on your original list of preferences when you did your application for a school place? If not why did you change?
- For late applications- why did you apply after the deadline?
- There are other schools in the area with places available, would you consider any of those?
- What is your back up plan if the Appeal was not granted? (Appeal Panels often ask this, it does not mean they are going to refuse the Appeal, but they are interested to hear what an appellant has to say for this question).

9 THE APPEAL HEARING

The Appeal Hearing

<u>Some points to help with the final preparations for your Appeal hearing</u>:

-The day before your Appeal hearing, make sure you have all your information / notes ready so that you are not worrying about finding them on the day.

-Double check the invitation letter for details of the time and location of your Appeal and make sure that you know how to get there in good time. If your Appeal is being run in the Grouped Method, you should have been given two appointment times (possibly on different dates)

- Take the invitation letter with you so that if there was an unforeseen delay in your journey you could telephone to let the Admission Authority know so that your Appeal was not held in your absence.

- Try to get to the venue a little earlier than your appointment time. This will give you a chance to catch your breath and settle before your Appeal hearing.

<u>Some points to help with the Appeal hearing itself</u>:

- Try not to be too nervous! It is a daunting experience, but all the people involved (Appeal Panel, Clerk, Presenting Officer) will try their best to put you at your ease.

- Sometimes Appeals run late. This can then have a knock on effect on Appeals afterwards. This is frustrating, but not the Clerk or Appeal Panel's fault, it can happen for many reasons. The Clerk should keep you updated and will be working to try to ensure that everyone is heard as soon as possible. Do not worry if your Appeal starts late, it should be conducted in the same way as it would have been if it had started on time and you should not feel rushed.

- If there is anything you don't understand in the Appeal hearing, ask! It is very important that you understand how your Appeal worked and the Panel should be happy for something to be explained to you if you are unsure.

- Try to stay calm. Don't interrupt the Presenting Officer whilst they are presenting their case, you will have the opportunity to ask any questions after they have presented their case and will be able to raise points which you feel are relevant when you are presenting your case. Remember the decision not to offer your child a place was not personal and the Presenting Officer may not have been involved in the allocations process at all.

- Remember the Appeal Panel need to follow their set procedure for deciding on an Appeal so they have to make the decision in the order explained earlier in this book. In the case of Class Size Appeals, it is the law that restricts them in the grounds on which they can uphold an Appeal.

- Sometimes parents get upset at their Appeal hearings. This won't affect your chances of winning your Appeal. Panel Members and the other people involved in the Appeal realise how important the Appeal is. They are used to appellants becoming emotional from time to time and will try to help by perhaps offering a glass of water or if necessary can adjourn the Appeal for a few minutes to allow the appellant to have a break before resuming.

- Try not to worry about forgetting to say something that you wish the Appeal Panel to consider as part of your case. If you have brought a list of your points with you this will help you not to miss anything out. You will have two opportunities to make your case so if you forget to say something when you are asked to tell the Appeal Panel why you feel your child should have a place at the school, you will have another chance at the end when you are asked to sum up your case. The Chair should ask you if you have said everything you wish to before they finish the Appeal Hearing.

10 AFTER THE APPEAL

Summary

You should be given an indication of when you will receive the decision of the Appeal Panel at the Appeal Hearing.

If you won your Appeal, you will need to contact the School to arrange when your child can start there.

If you didn't win your Appeal, you can remain on the Waiting List for a place at the School. You can reapply for a place and have a new Appeal in the next Academic Year, or earlier if you have a significant change of circumstances.

If you feel that your Appeal has not been carried out correctly you can complain to the Local Government Ombudsman or the Education Funding Authority depending on the type of school you were appealing for. Neither of these bodies can change the decision of the Appeal Panel, their role is to review the processes involved and if they feel that maladministration has occurred can recommend that another Appeal be allowed with a different Appeal Panel.

After the Appeal Hearing- finding out the decision

The Chair or Clerk should tell you in the Appeal hearing how and when the Appeal decision will be communicated to you. The Appeals Code states that you must receive the decision in writing, and that the decision letter includes the reasons for the decision that is made. The decision letter must be sent out within five school days of the Appeal hearing finishing. Remember that if your Appeal hearing is early on in a number of days of Appeals, this time scale is from the last day of Appeals so it could be a longer period of time to wait than if your Appeal was part of a single day of Appeals. You should be advised of the approximate date that you can expect your decision letter to arrive. Some Admission Authorities allow appellants to telephone to find out their decision before the letters are sent out, but many do not.

If you won your Appeal- Congratulations and what happens next

If you won your Appeal, your letter should inform you who you need to contact to arrange for your child to start at the School. Depending on if your appeal was an In Year appeal or for starting in Reception or Secondary School, the start date will vary. Sometimes the School's Admissions staff will telephone you to inform you that your Appeal was successful and to make arrangements for your child starting at the school. The Clerk will have informed the Local Education Authority of the outcome of all the Appeals heard.

If you didn't win your Appeal- What happens next

If your Appeal was unsuccessful, you may well be upset and disappointed. Try to stay calm and think about what you want to do next.

Waiting Lists

Your child should still be on the waiting list for the school you have appealed for. Depending on pupil movement, it is still possible that a place might become available. If this happens, the place will be allocated in line with the oversubscription criteria so if your child is at the top of the list when a place becomes available it should be offered to them. It is important to remember though that a place only becomes available when the number of children drops below the Published Admission Number. If a child has left a school but the year group had more than the Published Admission Number, this would not make a place available as the school would still be at or above the Published Admission Number. If a number of Appeals for the school were upheld, this would push the number of children above the Published Admission Number so it could take longer for a place to become available.

Can I appeal again?

You can appeal once every Academic Year. So if you wanted to you could wait and then Appeal again the following year. If you have a major change of circumstances, this can mean that you can have another Appeal earlier. It is up to the Admission Authority to determine what they consider to be a change of circumstances that would qualify for a new Appeal; however examples could include a house move or a sibling being offered a place at the school.

Can I complain?

If you are unhappy about the outcome of your Appeal, you can complain if you feel that the appeals process was done incorrectly in some way.

If your Appeal was for a community, foundation, voluntary aided or voluntary controlled school, you can complain to the Local Government Ombudsman – 0300 061 0614.

If your Appeal was for an Academy, you can complain to the Education Funding Agency – 0370 000 2288.

It is important to note that neither of these organisations have the power to change the Appeal Panel's decision. Their role is to review the way that the Admissions Authority and Appeal Panel dealt with your Appeal to determine if the requirements in terms of administering the Appeal correctly were met, and if the Appeal Panel took the relevant information into account in reaching its decision. If they investigate the case, they will review all of the documentation relating to it (refusal letter, appeal invitation letter, statement of case, the clerk's notes, and decision letter) and can also interview the Clerk and Chair if necessary.

If they do find some evidence of something going wrong in the appeal's process, they can recommend that the Admissions Authority allows you a new Appeal with a different Appeal Panel.

GLOSSARY

Admission Appeal	A hearing that can result in a child being offered a place at the school for which the Appeal is for if the Appeal is upheld.
Admission Authority	The body responsible for setting and applying the school's admission arrangements. For community and voluntary controlled schools, this is the local authority unless it has agreed to delegate responsibility to the governing body. For foundation or voluntary aided schools, this is the governing body of the school. For Academies, this is the Academy Trust.
Admission Arrangements	The overall procedure, practices and oversubscription criteria used in deciding the allocation of school places including any device or means used to determine whether a school place is to be offered.
Admission Number	The number of school places that the Admission Authority must offer in each relevant age group of a school for which it is the Admission Authority. Admission Numbers are part of a school's admission arrangements.

Appellant	The person / people who are Appealing for a place for their child at the school
Catchment area	A geographical area, from which children may be given priority for admission to a specific school. A catchment area is part of a school's admission arrangements.
Co-ordinated admission arrangements	The way in which Local Authorities co-ordinate the distribution of offers of places for schools in their area. All Local Authorities have to co-ordinate the normal admissions round for primary and secondary schools in their area.
Cut off distance	The distance from the school of the address of the last child to be offered a place in the normal admission round.
Education Funding Agency	The organisation who will investigate complaints about Appeals for Academies.

Education, Health and Care Plan	An Education, Health and Care plan is a plan made by the local authority under Section 37 of the Children and Families Act 2014 specifying the special education provision required for that child.
Excepted Child	The School Admissions (Infant Class Sizes) (England) Regulations 2012 allow children to be admitted as exceptions to the infant class size limit. These are detailed in Appendix A
Fair Access Protocol	A protocol that all Local Authorities must have. It has to be agreed with the majority of schools in the area and is meant to ensure that unplaced children, particularly the most vulnerable, outside the normal admission round are offered a school place as soon as possible. The mandatory categories are detailed in Appendix C.
Feeder School	A school named in the Admission Arrangements as one for whose pupils are afforded a priority in the oversubscription criteria.

Grouped (multiple) Appeals	Appeals usually for the normal admission round (Primary or Secondary schools) which are run so that all appellants are invited to hear the Admission Authority's case together, prior to their own individual appointments to present their case to the Appeal Panel. Multiple Appeals for the same school can run for a number of days.
In Year Appeal	An Appeal for a school place outside the normal admission round - not starting Primary or Secondary School but wishing to change schools at a different time or year group.
Infant Class Size Limit	Legislation limits the size of an infant class (a class in which the majority of children will reach the age of five, size or seven during the school year) to 30 pupils per school teacher.
Invitation Letter	The letter notifying the Appellant of their Appeal date and informing of the detailed arrangements such as time and location.
Legislation	Law governing School Admissions and School Admission Appeals.

Local Education Authority	The local councils who are responsible for administering the co-ordinated admission arrangements within their areas for school applications in the normal admission round.
Local Government Ombudsman	An independent, impartial and free service that investigates complaints about maladministration of certain public bodies.
Looked after child (and previously looked after children)	A 'looked after child' is a child who is (a) in the care of a local authority, or (b) being provided with accommodation by a local authority in the exercise of their social services functions (see the definition in Section 22(1) of the Children Act 1989) at the time of making an application to a school. Previously looked after children are children who were looked after, but ceased to be so because they were adopted (or became subject to a child arrangements order or special guardianship order.

National Offer Day	The day each year on which Local Authorities are required to send the offer of a school place to all parents of school pupils in their area. For secondary pupils, offers are sent out on 1st March. For primary pupils offers are sent out on 16th April.
Normal Admissions Round	The period during which parents are invited to express at least three preferences for a place at any state-funded school, in order of preference for children starting Reception or Secondary School. The deadlines for applications are 31st October for secondary school places and 15th January for Primary school places.
Oversubscription Oversubscribed	Where the number of applicants for places is higher than the school's published admission number.
Oversubscription Criteria	The published criteria that the Admission Authority applies when a school has more applications than places available in order to determine which children are offered places.

Prejudice	Being detrimental to something. In the case for Appeals – prejudicial to the school would mean detrimental to the school such as by reducing the standards at the school and the ability of the children already there to gain the best education possible.
Published Admission Number	The number of school places that the Admission Authority must offer in each relevant age group of a school for which it is the Admission Authority. Admission Numbers are part of a school's admission arrangements.
School Days	Days where the School would be open- usually Monday to Friday in term time. Weekends and school holidays do not count as school days. Some timescales within Appeals are measured in School Days.
Schools Adjudicator	A statutory office holder who is independent of but appointed by the Secretary of State. Decides on objections to published admission arrangements.

Statement of Case	The case put forward by the Admission Authority as to why they had to refuse the application for a place at the school and why they cannot admit any further children.
Statement of Special Educational Needs	A Statement of Special Educational Need is a statement made by the local authority under Section 324 of the Education Act 1996 specifying the special educational provision required for that child.
Topping up	This is a term used for the offers of places made to children on the waiting list for a school after the initial allocation of school places. If a place becomes available at a school then it is offered to the highest placed child on the waiting list by "topping up".
Waiting List	The list of children held and maintained by the Admission Authority when the school has allocated all of the places, on which the children are ranked in priority order against the school's published oversubscription criteria.

APPENDIX A

Exceptions to Class Size Legislation

(Section 2.15 of the School Admissions Code 2014)

Infant classes (those where the majority of children will reach the age of 5, 6 or 7 during the school year) must not contain more than 30 pupils with a single school teacher. Additional children may be admitted under limited exceptional circumstances. These children will remain an 'excepted pupil' for the time they are in an infant class or until the class numbers fall back to the current infant class size limit.

The excepted children are: a) children admitted outside the normal admissions round with statements of special educational needs or Education, Health and Care Plans specifying a school;

b) looked after children and previously looked after children admitted outside the normal admissions round;

c) children admitted, after initial allocation of places, because of a procedural error made by the admission authority or local authority in the original application process;

d) children admitted after an independent appeals panel upholds an appeal;

e) children who move into the area outside the normal admissions round for whom there is no other available school within reasonable distance;

f) children of UK service personnel admitted outside the normal admissions round;

g) children whose twin or sibling from a multiple birth is admitted otherwise than as an excepted pupil;

h) children with special educational needs who are normally taught in a special educational needs unit attached to the school, or registered at a special school, who attend some infant classes within the mainstream school.

APPENDIX B

School Admissions Code 2014 - How Admissions Work

"In summary, the process operates as follows:

a) All schools must have admission arrangements that clearly set out how children will be admitted, including the criteria that will be applied if there are more applications than places at the school. Admission arrangements are determined by admission authorities.

b) Admission authorities must set ('determine') admission arrangements annually. Where changes are proposed to admission arrangements, the admission authority must first publicly consult on those arrangements . If no changes are made to admission arrangements, they must be consulted on at least once every 7 years. For admission arrangements for entry in September 2016, consultation must be for a minimum of 8 weeks and must be completed by 1 March 2015. For all subsequent years, consultation must be for a minimum of 6 weeks and must take place between 1 October and 31 January of the school year before those arrangements are to apply. For example: for arrangements which are to apply to applications in 2016 (entry in September 2017), consultation must be completed by 31 January 2016. This consultation period allows parents, other schools, religious authorities and the local community to raise any concerns about proposed admission arrangements.

c) Once all arrangements have been determined, arrangements can be objected to and referred to the Schools Adjudicator. Objections to admission arrangements for entry in September 2016 must be referred to the Adjudicator by 30 June 2015. For all subsequent years, objections must be referred to the Adjudicator by 15 May in the determination year. Any decision of the Adjudicator must be acted on by the admission authority and admission arrangements amended accordingly. The local authority will collate and publish all the admission arrangements in the area in a single composite prospectus.

d) In the normal admissions round parents apply to the local authority in which they live for places at their preferred schools. Parents are able to express a preference for at least three schools. The application can include schools outside the local authority where the child lives: a parent can apply for a place for their child at any state-funded school in any area. If a school is undersubscribed, any parent that applies must be offered a place. When oversubscribed, a school's admission authority must rank applications in order against its published oversubscription criteria and send that list back to the local authority. Published admission arrangements must make clear to parents that a separate application must be made for any transfer from nursery to primary school, and from infant to junior school.

e) All preferences are collated and parents then receive an offer from the local authority at the highest preference school at which a place is available. For secondary schools, the offer is made on or about 1 March (known as National Offer Day) in the year in which the child will be admitted. For primary schools, the offer is made on or about 16 April, in the year in which the child will be admitted.

f) Parents, and in some circumstances children, have the right to appeal against an admission authority's decision to refuse admission. The admission authority must set out the reasons for the decision, that there is a right of appeal and the process for hearing such appeals. The admission authority must establish an independent appeals panel to hear the appeal. The panel will decide whether to uphold or dismiss the appeal. Where a panel upholds the appeal the school is required to admit the child."

APPENDIX C

Mandatory categories of the Fair Access Protocol (from The School Admissions Code 2014)

"The list of children to be included in a Fair Access Protocol is to be agreed with the majority of schools in the area but must, as a minimum, include the following children of compulsory school age who have difficulty securing a school place:

a) children from the criminal justice system or Pupil Referral Units who need to be reintegrated into mainstream education;

b) children who have been out of education for two months or more;

c) children of Gypsies, Roma, Travellers, refugees and asylum seekers;

d) children who are homeless;

e) children with unsupportive family backgrounds for whom a place has not been sought;

f) children who are carers; and

g) children with special educational needs, disabilities or medical conditions (but without a statement or Education, Health and Care Plan). "

ABOUT THE AUTHOR

The author has extensive experience working in School Appeals, from clerking individual School Appeals to being responsible for the overall running and co-ordination of the School Appeals Service of a large Local Authority. The author now runs their own Admission Appeal Clerking Service and is also an experienced Independent Admission Appeals Member.

Printed in Great Britain
by Amazon